INTERNATIONAL HUMAN RIGHTS,
SOCIETY,
AND THE SCHOOLS

NATIONAL COUNCIL FOR THE SOCIAL STUDIES BULLETIN NO. 68

International Human Rights, Society, and the Schools

Margaret Stimmann Branson and

Judith Torney-Purta

Editors

Library of Congress Catalog Card Number 82-60695
ISBN 0-87986-044-8
Copyright © 1982 by the
NATIONAL COUNCIL FOR THE SOCIAL STUDIES
3501 Newark Street, N.W., Washington, DC 20016

095374

CONTENTS

About the Authors   vi

Foreword   viii

Acknowledgments   xi

International Human Rights: Significant Events and Documents   xii

Introduction   1
    Margaret Stimmann Branson and Judith Torney-Purta

1. **International Human Rights: A Primer**   7
    Margaret Stimmann Branson

2. **International Human Rights and Civic Education**   23
    R. Freeman Butts

3. **Socialization and Human Rights Research:**
   Implications for Teachers   35
    Judith Torney-Purta

4. **Human Rights in Elementary and Middle Schools**   49
    Charlotte C. Anderson

5. **Teaching Human Rights in Secondary Schools**   61
    David C. King and Sharon Flitterman-King

6. **International Human Rights Education:**
   The Challenge for Colleges and Universities   71
    Jan L. Tucker

7. **Reading and "Righting":**
   Books About Human Rights for Children and Youth   81
    Margaret Stimmann Branson

Appendix   97

Index   109

ABOUT THE AUTHORS

CHARLOTTE C. ANDERSON is Assistant Staff Director of the Special Committee on Youth Education for Citizenship of the American Bar Association. She has taught at the elementary and university levels and has conducted many inservice workshops throughout the United States. She is the author of books and articles in both law-related education and global education.

MARGARET STIMMANN BRANSON, coeditor of this Bulletin, is History/Social Science Consultant, Office of Kern County Superintendent of Schools, Bakersfield, California. She has been Associate Professor of Education and Human Development at Holy Names College, and Director of Secondary Education at Mills College, Oakland, California. The author of numerous articles and textbooks, she received the Hilda Taba Award as "a distinguished education leader who has made a significant contribution to the Social Studies" in 1973, and a Delta Kappa Gamma International Scholarship in 1980–1981.

R. FREEMAN BUTTS is a Fellow of the Charles F. Kettering Foundation for work in civic literacy and civic education and a visiting scholar in the Hoover Institution of Stanford University. He is William F. Russell Professor Emeritus in the Foundations of Education, Teachers College, Columbia University, where he was for many years Director of the Institute for International Studies. His most recent books are *The Revival of Civic Learning* (Phi Delta Kappa Educational Foundation, 1980) and *Public Education in the United States* (Holt, Rinehart and Winston, 1978).

SHARON FLITTERMAN-KING, a Staff Associate with Global Perspectives in Education, Inc., is currently on the faculty at Simon's Rock of Bard College, Annandale-on-Hudson, New York. She holds a Ph.D. in English Literature from the University of California, Berkeley, where she taught English. She has also taught in the Bard College Workshops in Language and Thinking, and she is the developer of curriculum materials in both the social studies and the humanities.

DAVID C. KING is Senior Editor for Global Perspectives in Education, Inc. He has developed multimedia packages, and he is the author of numerous articles and textbooks. Among his more recent textbooks are *America: Past and Present* (in the Houghton Mifflin series *Windows On*

Our World), *Cultures,* and *Peoples of the World* (American Book Company), and a forthcoming high-school American history (to be published by Addison-Wesley Publishing Company).

JUDITH TORNEY-PURTA, coeditor of this Bulletin, is Professor of Human Development at the University of Maryland at College Park. Prior to her appointment at Maryland, she was Professor of Psychology at the University of Illinois at Chicago. For six years she was a member of the United States National Commission for UNESCO, representing the Social Science Education Consortium. She held the Office of Vice-Chair of the Commission and Chair of the Human Rights Committee. In 1977, she received the National Council for the Social Studies Citation for Exemplary Research for her analysis of the development of political attitudes.

JAN L. TUCKER is Professor of Social Studies Education at Florida International University, Miami, Florida. He serves on the Board of Directors of the National Council for the Social Studies and has represented NCSS on the United States National Commission for UNESCO since 1977.

FOREWORD

Every human being wants to live in dignity. Human rights are those rights which every man, woman, and child has by birthright to live a dignified life that is free of poverty, illiteracy, and cultural and political repression. People become dehumanized to the extent that they lose opportunities to live dignified lives with protections for basic human rights. One of the most important characteristics that distinguishes humans from other beings on earth is their ability to create cultures that regard human life as sacred and that promote human dignity and creativity.

Today our world is one of paradox. While we are experiencing phenomenal technological growth, there are ominous threats to human rights and human welfare. Nuclear weapons—the offspring of modern science—seriously threaten human survival. Their destructive potential is beyond human imagination. Poverty, hunger, limited wars, authoritarian governments, apartheid, illiteracy, and international terror also present serious threats to human rights. The problems posed by such threats are intractable and overwhelming. Yet, as social studies educators and human beings, we have an inescapable responsibility to do what we can to help solve them and to improve the human condition.

It is far easier to affirm our commitment to improve human rights in the world than to take actions that will achieve this goal. It is very difficult to enforce international human rights pronouncements and laws. Some very significant documents, such as the Universal Declaration of Human Rights, and the International Covenant on Civil and Political Rights, are designed to protect human rights throughout the world. However, it is often difficult for nations committed to the protection of these rights to bring sanctions successfully against nations that violate them. Often, citizens and groups within nations focus on their unique concerns and demonstrate little interest in the rights of other citizens within their own or other nations.

A major challenge that we face in international human rights is how to create an international constituency (in different nations) that is not only committed to the protection of human rights throughout the world, but that also can effectively mobilize to bring decisive sanctions against nations that consistently violate those rights. Strong commitments to community and nation-state and a tendency to focus on particularistic issues often prevent citizens and groups from taking actions related to global issues and concerns.

It is essential for a nation's citizens to experience equity and human rights before they can realistically be expected to participate in actions to protect the human rights of other people within or outside their national borders. Citizens who are struggling to survive, who are illiterate, who feel that they have few basic rights, or who are structurally excluded from their own polity are likely to show little interest in the human rights of other groups. Consequently, the most important contribution that social studies educators can make to promoting international human rights is to help create conditions in social and political institutions that promote equity and human rights and that help students to see how their own human rights are inextricably bound up in the human rights of other peoples throughout the world.

Violations of human rights in one nation usually have important consequences in others. When Haitian and Cuban refugees fled from their nations to the United States, they had a significant impact on the Miami area and exacerbated ethnic conflict. The Mexicans who cross the Rio Grande seeking jobs in the United States affect jobs and educational opportunities for Americans, especially for Mexican Americans. Yet, citizens who are preoccupied with protecting and attaining their own basic rights often do not see the interrelationship between their rights and those of other world citizens.

As the difficulties involved in enforcing international human rights make clear (witness the fate of President Carter's human rights policy), we can best protect human rights in the international community only when a critical mass of citizens throughout the world is committed to their protection and when these citizens are able to mobilize for effective social and political action.

To help future citizens develop a commitment to international human rights, we must create situations in their communities, schools, and nations in which they are treated with dignity and equity. Educators can best contribute to the promotion of international human rights by creating a school environment that respects the human rights of students. The school, wrote John Dewey, should be a model democracy. Human rights should be promoted, exemplified, and protected in the school. Within this kind of atmosphere, the teaching of the concepts of international human rights will make sense to students because their experiences will be consistent with what they are being taught. Attempts to teach and promote human rights in an authoritarian atmosphere will be rightfully dismissed by students as empty rhetoric and hypocrisy.

This thoughtful and well-written Bulletin is a rich and stimulating resource for teachers interested in teaching about international human rights and protecting the rights of students. It discusses important issues, concepts, and research related to international human rights. It also includes useful instructional guidelines and creative teaching strategies.

I am deeply grateful to Margaret Stimmann Branson and Judith Torney-Purta for contributing to this Bulletin and for serving as co-editors, and I wish to thank the other authors for their contributions. I am also grateful to Dan Roselle and Howard Langer and their staff for carefully preparing this Bulletin for publication.

James A Banks, *President*
National Council for the Social Studies

ACKNOWLEDGMENTS

The United States National Commission for the United Nations Educational, Scientific and Cultural Organization, better known as the U.S. National Commission for UNESCO, is a 100-member body of individuals and nongovernmental organizations created by the Congress in 1946 to advise the United States government on matters relating to UNESCO and to promote an understanding of the objectives of UNESCO among the people of the United States. Similar Commissions exist in nearly all the member countries of UNESCO. The Commission relies upon its members, acting as private citizens, to advise the government on UNESCO programs and to inform individuals and groups in the United States about UNESCO activities. The National Council for the Social Studies has been represented on the Commission for many years; its current representative is Jan Tucker.

The budget of the U.S. National Commission for UNESCO has provided some financial support for this publication as part of its attempts to familiarize the American educational community with the 1974 UNESCO Recommendation on Education for International Understanding, Cooperation and Peace and Education Relating to Human Rights and Fundamental Freedoms.

We also wish to express our appreciation to the Meiklejohn Civil Liberties Institute of Berkeley, California, and to Professor Ann Fagan-Ginger for assistance in securing the graphics that appear in this book Meiklejohn Civil Liberties Institute is a public-interest law center serving the national community by answering queries, by publishing material on current constitutional questions, and by preserving invaluable materials on civil rights, civil liberties, due process, and labor law.

Our thanks, too, to Ben Goldstein for his artistic selection of the graphics used in this Bulletin and to the Ben and Beatrice Goldstein Foundation of New York City, which has made possible their use.

The cover picture is a photograph by J.C. Constant of a Nicaraguan child in a Honduras refugee camp. It is supplied courtesy of the U.N. High Commissioner on Refugees.

INTERNATIONAL HUMAN RIGHTS: SIGNIFICANT EVENTS AND DOCUMENTS*

DATE	EVENT OR DOCUMENT
1941	Atlantic Charter In January 1942 a number of nations also agreed to work for a world in which people may "live out their lives in freedom from fear and want."
1945	United Nations Charter Preamble "reaffirm[s] faith in fundamental human rights, in the dignity and worth of the human person, in the equal rights of men and women and of nations large and small." Articles 1, 13, 55, 56, 62, 68, and 76 accentuate human rights. *First UN Yearbook on Human Rights* Member states report progress in field of human rights.
1948	Universal Declaration of Human Rights The first and most fundamental formulation of international human rights standards is proclaimed by the UN General Assembly. Convention on the Prevention and Punishment of the Crime of Genocide
1950	European Convention on Human Rights (entered into force in 1953)
1952	Convention on the Political Rights of Women
1959	Declaration of the Rights of the Child
1961	U.S. Congress passes Foreign Assistance Act Requires annual written reports on human rights from nations receiving American aid.
1963	Declaration on the Elimination of All Forms of Racial Discrimination
1966	International Bill of Human Rights completed with additions of: • International Covenant on Civil and Political Rights • International Covenant on Economic, Social, and Cultural Rights • Optional Protocol to International Covenant on Civil and Political Rights
1969	American Convention on Human Rights, "Pact of San José, Costa Rica" (entered into force in 1978)
1971	Declaration on the Rights of Mentally Retarded Persons
1974	UNESCO Recommendation Concerning Education for International Understanding, Cooperation and Peace and Education Relating to Human Rights and Fundamental Freedoms

*Prepared by Margaret Stimmann Branson.

1975   The Helsinki Accord

Declaration of the Rights of Disabled Persons

Declaration on the Use of Scientific and Technological Progress

Declaration on the Protection Against Torture and Other Cruel, Inhuman or Degrading Treatment or Punishment

1976   International Covenants on Civil and Political Rights and on Economic, Social, and Cultural Rights take effect (35 and 37 signatories respectively)

1977   United States signs International Covenants on Civil and Political Rights and on Economic, Social, and Cultural Rights in special ceremony at UN headquarters.

United States signs American Convention on Human Rights

Amnesty International is awarded Nobel Peace Prize for its work on behalf of Prisoners of Conscience

1978   International Covenants on Civil and Political Rights and on Economic, Social, and Cultural Rights are sent to U.S. Senate for Approval

UNESCO asks member states to take stock of world situation in respect to teaching of Human Rights

First World Congress on the Teaching of Human Rights is held in Vienna under UNESCO auspices

1979   U.S. Congress amends Foreign Assistance Act, expands coverage of annual human rights report to all countries which are UN members

1980   U.S. State Department Report to Congress on Human Rights proclaims: "There now exists an international consensus that recognizes basic human rights and obligations owed by all governments to their citizens . . .
- the right to be free from governmental violations of the integrity of the person . . .
- the right to the fulfillment of vital needs such as food, shelter, health care, and education . . .
- the right to enjoy civil and political liberties . . ."

1981   Office of UN High Commissioner for Refugees is awarded Nobel Peace Prize for its aid to 10 million of the world's estimated 14-18 million refugees

Amnesty International marks its 20th Anniversary by denouncing violations of human rights by at least 60 UN member states and calling for universal ratification of International Human Rights Covenants

Freedom House survey claims repression of human rights is increasing throughout the world

1982   Intergovernmental meeting to assess the Implementation of the 1974 UNESCO Recommendation on Education for International Understanding, Cooperation and Peace and Education Relating to Human Rights and Fundamental Freedoms

UNIVERSAL DECLARATION OF HUMAN RIGHTS

All human beings should act toward one another in a spirit of brotherhood

Article 1.　All human beings are born free and equal in dignity and rights. They are endowed with reason and conscience and should act towards one another in a spirit of brotherhood.

Article 29.　(1) Everyone has duties to the community in which alone the free and full development of his personality is possible.

Article 28.　Everyone is entitled to a social and international order in which the rights and freedoms set forth in this Declaration can be fully realized.

Untitled, Packard, 1914-　. USA. Ink drawing made for the program of the first performance of "A Human Rights Cantata" by James F. Wood.

INTRODUCTION

Margaret Stimmann Branson and
Judith Torney-Purta

As a professional organization, the National Council for the Social Studies can be proud of its record of dedication to education in the broad, but related fields of human rights and international understanding. Over the years NCSS has concerned itself with human rights, most notably in the domestic context. Through its publications program and other means, NCSS has done much to improve teaching and learning about the United States Constitution and its Bill of Rights. It has accorded continuing and deserved attention to law-related education as a means by which citizens can learn how the liberties and justice promised in those fundamental documents can be more generally secured. NCSS also has called attention to the needs of particular individuals and groups whose rights have not always been respected because of their sex, ethnic origin, or religion, or because of the unpopularity of their views.

Along with its concern for human rights and law-related education, NCSS has manifested an abiding interest in international understanding. It has sponsored conferences on global education and published a wide variety of Bulletins and Yearbooks in the transnational field.

In view of the record just cited, this new Bulletin is an appropriate and logical step for NCSS, taken in cooperation with the United States National Commission for UNESCO and its Committee on Human Rights. In a sense, this publication brings together parallel perspectives in education and calls attention to what is perhaps the most consequential agenda item of our time: international human rights. Throughout the world, men and women are yearning for recognition of their inherent dignity as human beings. They are pressing claims for international equity, along with claims for domestic justice. They are challenging practices and regimes which they believe contravene their human rights, those rights to which they are entitled, not because of nationality, wealth, or gender, but by virtue of the fact that they are human beings. They are appealing for help to international bodies and to the conscience of the world. All of these events taken together add up to a new climate, a new insistence on respect for human dignity and new urgencies to which educators must be attentive. Those urgencies have special meaning for social studies educators, who bear particular and inescapable responsibilities in the broad field of citizenship education and for the promotion of international understanding. Social studies teachers need to teach their students about human rights, to elevate the level of discussion and debate about them, and to equip their students with the intellectual and participatory skills necessary for taking appropriate actions. Many social studies teachers already have accepted responsibilities for human rights education, but they often stop short of providing the kind of broad education in international human rights which now is needed.

Three Basic Approaches to the Study of Human Rights

There are three basic approaches to the study of rights—the national, the comparative, and the international. While the national approach is commonly employed in the United States in elementary and secondary schools, not all teachers are conscious of the fact that they are teaching about human rights. Just as a character in a play discovered, with a start, that he had been speaking prose all his life, some teachers—particularly those who teach American history and government—might be startled to be told that they really are teaching basic human rights concepts and that the textbooks they are using give extensive coverage to human rights. Both teachers and textbooks, however, tend to confine their attention to human rights on the national scene.

Certainly, it is important that students learn about rights in the context of their nation's history and about the rights guaranteed by the United States Constitution. Indeed, many persons today argue that students presently are not learning in sufficient depth about rights in the American context. On the other hand, there are those who contend that students are not learning about rights with sufficient breadth. The argument to be made in this Bulletin is that if students study human rights in the national setting only, they will develop a narrow perspective, one which may not serve them very well as adult citizens in an increasingly interdependent world.

A second alternative is the comparative approach to the study of human rights. This approach necessitates the study of other nations; their constitutions, whether written or unwritten; the rights guaranteed to their citizens; and the degree to which those rights are in fact being enjoyed.

There are advantages to the comparative approach. One important advantage is that students will come to realize that although human rights are important to peoples everywhere, different societies do not necessarily agree on which rights are of greatest importance. In Western Europe and the United States, for example, civil and political rights such as freedom of speech, voting, and due process are of prime concern. In Eastern European countries, economic rights such as the right to work, to form trade unions, to strike, and to take vacations are considered essential. In Asian and African countries, social and cultural rights such as the right to be free from hunger, the right to education, and the right of an ethnic group to its own language are emphasized. The rights which are deemed most important depend upon the social, economic, legal, and political traditions of the people. Even so, there is common agreement among the peoples of the world that the rights enunciated in the Universal Declaration of Human Rights are of consequence and should be observed.

A second advantage of the comparative approach is that it can provide balance. It can guard against students believing that Americans are the only people in the world whose Constitution deals with rights. It can direct attention to economic, social, and cultural rights, as well as to civil and political rights. The comparative approach does have potential pitfalls, however. If the only countries chosen for study are those which are violators of human rights, students may in fact have their nationalistic biases and stereotypes reinforced.

A third way of approaching the study of human rights is an international approach. This approach centers attention on those international, regional, and nongovernmental organizations which are concerned with the protection of human rights. It is an approach that deserves attention, because it can link the national and comparative approaches, enrich the understanding of basic human needs and the search for dignity, and put the concept of rights in a global perspective.

The international approach is of more recent origin. Prior to World War II, international law left nations very free to treat their citizens as they wished. However oppressive they might be, measures taken by a government against its own nationals were considered to be within the government's domestic jurisdiction. Other governments could not lodge formal complaints to international bodies about those oppressive measures. The world's horror at the Holocaust, in particular, stimulated a desire among the community of nations to change the situation which allowed the inhumanity of governments to go unchallenged. That desire led to the birth of the United Nations, the institution of the UN Charter, and the adoption of the Universal Declaration of Human Rights in 1948. Those two documents, the UN Charter and the Universal Declaration of Human Rights, established the first standards for international human rights. They provided a yardstick or the criteria by which adherence to the agreed-upon standard could be measured. In addition, they led to the establishment of international, regional, and nongovernmental bodies concerned with monitoring the observance of human rights.

Many of these international, regional, and nongovernmental organizations regard the education of both young people and adults as an important—even as an essential—part of their work. UNESCO, to cite one example, is committed to the belief that real peace in the world can only be built upon respect for human rights and that education is the key to engendering that respect. UNESCO also believes that it is important to begin early to build respect for human rights. Just as citizenship education with a national focus cannot be deferred until the adult years, neither can human rights education with an international focus be postponed.

The 1974 UNESCO Recommendation on Education

Because of the importance placed on education and a growing desire to recognize its importance in a concrete manner, UNESCO adopted at its General Conference of 1974 a Recommendation Concerning Education for International Understanding, Cooperation and Peace and Education Relating to Human Rights and Fundamental Freedoms. UNESCO, of course, has been active for many years in programs of education designed to promote international understanding. The 1974 Recommendation, however, marked the first time that human rights were explicitly linked to those programs. Not only did that linkage stimulate new interest in UNESCO's educational aims, it recognized that peace, understanding between peoples of different countries, and respect for human rights are inextricably bound together. The Recommendation, a relatively brief statement, enunciates some general principles and makes some specific suggestions for their implementation. The Recommendation was sent to all nations which are members of UNESCO. In the United States, the Recommendation has served to highlight the importance of incorporating human rights education into the many programs for international understanding and global education which already are in existence. More, however, needs to be done to expand those programs and to see that they include the study of human rights by all students at all grade levels in all schools.

Why Human Rights Education?

There are compelling reasons for educating American students in human rights in this the last quarter of the twentieth century. There also are compelling reasons for not confining that education to a national approach. Human rights education should incorporate the comparative and international approaches as well as the national, if it is to be adequate to our time.

• First, the study of human rights illuminates the human condition and stresses the universality of the search for human dignity. A recent survey of elementary school curricula indicates that because attempts to make students aware of cultural differences are so pervasive, students may not realize that all human beings have common basic needs and that they share common aspirations. Certainly, the study of human rights in a more global context could correct such misconceptions.

- Second, to be effective citizens, students need to understand human rights in all three contexts: national, comparative, and international. One cannot understand the foreign policy of one's own government or that of other governments apart from understanding the struggle for human rights. Further, when young people become adult citizens, they will have an enormous potential impact on the policies of government as members of the body of public opinion. They also will have opportunities through nongovernmental organizations to which they belong to make an impact on policy decisions. As consumers, producers, and members of professional, political, religious, civic, and charitable groups, they will help to determine policies and affect the course of world events.
- Third, human rights represent a field of knowledge which can serve as an organizing framework, as well as providing substance or content for global studies. In the past, global studies sometimes have lacked substance and focus. Problems such as hunger, for example, have been studied in isolation. As a result, students sometimes have come away from such study believing that developed countries should come to the aid of underdeveloped countries, in a spirit of charity, rather than realizing that the right to freedom from hunger is a basic human right to which every human being is entitled.
- Finally, the study of specific human rights documents, such as the Universal Declaration, the Covenants on Civil and Political Rights and on Economic, Social, and Cultural Rights, and the Declaration of the Rights of the Child, can do much to dissipate students' egocentric and ethnocentric views of rights. Contrary to popular belief, a person's desire to do something and the right to do it are not the same. An individual cannot violate the rights of another and justify the violation on the basis of personal preference. The existence of rights, under law, connotes corresponding duties towards others. Young people need to develop a deeper appreciation of the relationship of rights and duties. They also need to realize that human rights and the corresponding duties they entail are not the birthright of the few. Human rights are the birthright of all — of every man, woman, and child in the world today.

UNIVERSAL DECLARATION OF HUMAN RIGHTS

The right to freedom of opinion and expression

Article 19.   Everyone has the right to freedom of opinion and expression; this right includes freedom to hold opinions without interference and to seek, receive and impart information and ideas through any media and regardless of frontiers.

Homage to José Guadalupe Posada.
Leopoldo, Méndez. 1902–1969. Mexico. Linocut. Collection of Ben Goldstein.

Chapter 1

INTERNATIONAL HUMAN RIGHTS: A PRIMER

Margaret Stimmann Branson

The following answers to fifteen questions often asked about international human rights are presented to provide a basis for subsequent chapters in this Bulletin:

1. What ARE Human Rights — And What Are They Not?

Human rights are those rights which belong to every man, woman, and child simply because each of them is a person, a human being. They are rights which exist prior to and independent of governments.[1] Human rights, therefore, are rights which are inalienable.

Another way to explain what human rights *are* is to explain what they are *not*. Human rights are not a very recent discovery, a passing concern, an ephemeral issue. Human rights are not something about which only people in the Western World care. Neither are human rights "a new morality" or a "lay religion."[2] On the contrary, "human rights are claims asserted and recognized 'as of right,' not claims upon love, or grace, or brotherhood, or charity; one does not have to earn or deserve them. They are not merely aspirations or moral assertions, but increasingly, legal claims under some applicable law."[3]

Most prominent among those "applicable laws" are four significant documents: the United Nations Charter, the Universal Declaration of Human Rights, the International Covenant on Economic, Social, and Cultural Rights, and the International Covenant on Civil and Political Rights. These documents and others identify and describe specific

[1]U.S. Department of State, Bureau of Public Affairs. Current Policy No. 353, "Double Standards in Human Rights," A statement by Ambassador Jeane J. Kirkpatrick, U.S. Permanent Representative to the United Nations, before the Third Committee, United Nations General Assembly, New York, November 24, 1981.

[2]UNESCO's Medium Term Plan (1977–1982) cited in Karel Vasak, "Human Rights: A New School of Law and Learning," *The UNESCO Courier* (October, 1978), p. 6.

[3]Louis Henkin, *The Rights of Man Today* (Boulder, Colorado: Westview Press, 1978), pp. 1–2.

human rights ranging from rights to work, to rest and to have leisure, to be educated, and to take part in the government of one's country.

Human rights, in sum, are more than abstractions, more than theoretical legal or philosophical concepts. Human rights are the birthright of every person, because each man, woman, and child has inherent dignity and each is a member of the human family.

2. When and Where Did Ideas of Human Rights Originate?

Pinpointing either the time or the place of origin of ideas about human rights is impossible. There is evidence that concern for human rights dates back many centuries. That evidence can be read in the records of the world's earliest civilizations which speak to matters of right and wrong, good and evil, law, legality, and illegality. Further evidence can be found in the teachings of all of the major religions, as well as in the writings of philosophers from diverse lands.

Early philosophers often couched their interest in human rights in terms such as "the higher law" or "natural law." They contended that natural law was common to all humankind. It was both the source and the standard of political right. In time, ideas of natural law developed into beliefs about natural rights. During the eighteenth century, those beliefs were set forth explicitly in the Declarations which emerged during the American Revolution and the French Revolution.

In succeeding centuries, recognition of human rights has been incorporated in constitutions of states on every continent. That is not to say, of course, that pledges to respect human rights have been honored. In all too many instances, they have not. However, it is clear that concern for human rights is not a new invention, nor is it the concern only of Americans or of Western Europeans.

3. Why Have Human Rights Become a Central Issue for All Humankind?

Concern for human rights, although not new, has emerged as a central issue for all humankind with rather dramatic suddenness. Today there is almost no place in the world where awareness of human rights has not penetrated. That is due in part to the activities of international organizations which have helped establish standards for human rights which can be applied across countries, to the intense focus of the media on human rights, and to increased awareness of human rights by peoples all over the world. The awareness, furthermore, no longer is limited to better educated persons, to policy-making elites, or to those who live in democratic societies.

Human rights issues have emerged as major agenda items for discussion not only in regional and international organizations; they are also major agenda items among labor, religious, professional, and civic groups. Human rights have become a subject of active national policy debate in country after country. Individuals and groups are challenging practices and regimes which they believe fail to respect their human rights. There is, in short, a new climate, a new insistence on respect for human dignity.

4. What Evidence Exists of the Need for Attention to Human Rights?

Our age is paradoxical. It is a time of unprecedented advances in medicine, science, technology, and communication. It also is a time of widespread oppression, increased strife, and callous disregard for human life in many quarters of the world. Consider the following facts and estimates, drawn from the work of reputable scholars and organizations:

- Over a billion people — one fourth of the world's population — live below "the absolute poverty line."[4]
- In this century alone, over one hundred million people have fallen victim to wars.[5]
- The number of refugees is placed at somewhere between 8.1 and 10.9 million. Persons are fleeing their homes in 37 different countries, and the future outlook is for a continued heavy flow.[6]
- Twice as many governments today are authoritarian as are democratic. "Death squads" tacitly or openly approved by governments kidnap and kill students, labor leaders, lawyers, journalists, business persons, or others who threaten their claims to power.[7]
- Not only is the use of torture widespread, but there is also a new subculture of terror. "Advanced" technology enables a captor to break a prisoner's will in a matter of hours while leaving no mark.[8]
- In South Africa the system of *apartheid* not only denies basic human rights to more than 19 million Blacks, 2.5 million Coloreds, and some 800,000 Asians, but also it restricts the freedom of the 4.5 million Whites who also live there.[9]
- Hunger is chronic in many parts of the world. Some 70 million are in immediate danger of starving to death. As many as 400 to 600

---

[4] Remarks of the Rev. Theodore M. Hesburgh, Chairman of the American Delegation to the UN Conference on Science and Technology, as reported in "Vienna Notebook," *The Chronicle of Higher Education,* Vol. XX, No. 2, 10 September 1979, p. 4.

[5] *Ibid.*

[6] U.S. Library of Congress Study, as reported by the Associated Press. *San Francisco Chronicle,* 23 June 1979, p. 14. See, also, *UNHRC: News From the U.N. Commissioner For Refugees,* No. 3, June/July, 1978, p. 2.

[7] Report of Freedom House, cited in Vogelgesang.

[8] *Ibid.*

[9] Figures taken from Leslie Rubin, "South Africa: Facts and Fiction," *The UNESCO Courier,* Nov., 1977, p. 9.

million are estimated to be suffering from brain deficiencies on account of inadequate nutrition.[10]

- In "less developed" nations, not even half of the males ages 12–17 are enrolled in school. Less than one-fourth of the females in that age group are in school.[11]

- One adult in four in the world is unable to read and write. While the latest forecasts indicate that the illiteracy rate will have fallen by 1990, the absolute number of illiterates is expected to increase in the same period from 742 million to 814 million.[12]

- Between 1951 and 1971, the United Nations received 120,000 complaints from individuals and groups that alleged that their human rights had been violated and that they had exhausted all domestic sources for remedy. Since 1971, the Commission on Human Rights and its Subcommission on Prevention of Discrimination and Protection of Minorities has considered over 20,000 individual communications in certain years.[13]

Many more facts and figures could be provided. These data serve only to suggest the magnitude of human rights violations in the world today.

5. Why Should International Human Rights Be of Especial Concern to the People of the United States?

There are at least three very good reasons why the people of the United States should be especially concerned about international human rights.

First, concern about human rights is in the American tradition and at the core of the American creed. The government of the United States was founded squarely and explicitly on the belief that the primary purpose of government is to secure and protect the rights of its citizens. Certainly, the Declaration of Independence makes that abundantly clear:

We hold these Truths to be self-evident, that all Men are created equal, that they are endowed by their Creator with certain unalienable Rights, that among these are Life, Liberty, and the Pursuit of Happiness—That to secure these Rights, Governments are instituted among Men, deriving their just Powers from the Consent of the Governed . . . .

---

[10]See Michael Harrington, *The Vast Majority: A Journey to the World's Poor* (New York: Simon and Schuster, 1977). See, also, Roger Lewin, "Starved Brains," *Psychology Today,* Vol. 9, No. 4 (September, 1975), pp. 29–33. Lewin, a British science writer, is Science Editor for *The New Scientist.*

[11]"World's Children Data Sheet of the Population Reference Bureau, Inc.," 1979.

[12]*News From UNESCO.* A Bulletin published by the Office of Public Information, UNESCO (7 Place de Fontenoy 75700, Paris, France, October, 1978), p. iv.

[13]Louis B. Sohn, "The Improvement of the UN Machinery on Human Rights," *International Studies Quarterly,* Vol. 23, No. 2, June, 1979, p. 203.

The United States Constitution makes the commitment of Americans to human rights even more explicit. Time and again, words such as "the right of the people" and "the right of citizens" appear in its text. So, too, do the words "Congress shall make no law," which make it clear that not even the highest legislative authority can abridge the rights of the people.

Second, the United States has played a key role in helping to establish, support, and maintain the United Nations. The Charter of that organization commits its members, of which the United States is one, to the promotion of "universal respect for the observance of human rights and fundamental freedoms for all."

Third, the United States has continued to assume responsibilities for the promotion of international human rights. It would be an impossible task to provide here an exhaustive list of the international obligations of the United States in the field of human rights. An abbreviated accounting of its major obligations, however, reveals that:

- The United States has ratified the UN Charter.
- The United States subscribes to the Universal Declaration of Human Rights.
- The United States is a member of the Organization of American States (OAS). It has signed the American Convention on Human Rights (the "Pact of San José"). Ratification currently is pending in the United States Senate.
- The United States has signed the International Covenant on Civil and Political Rights. Ratification currently is pending in the United States Senate.
- The United States has signed the International Covenant on Economic, Social, and Cultural Rights. Ratification currently is pending in the United States Senate.
- The United States has ratified conventions for the suppression of slavery, the treatment of refugees, and the political rights of women.
- The United States has signed the Helsinki Agreement, thereby promising to "respect, promote, and encourage" the "effective exercise of civil, political, economic, social, cultural and other rights and freedoms all of which derive from the inherent dignity of the human person and are essential for his free and full development."

Certainly, it is true that there are other human rights conventions to which the United States has not become a party. Some nations have accepted more of them than has the United States. Nonetheless, the basic orientation of Americans and the historic thrust of the United States reflect a deep-seated concern for human rights in both the national and international arenas.

6. What Does the United Nations Charter Say About Human Rights?

One of the most remarkable developments in the establishment of international human rights came as World War II was drawing to a close. In April, 1945, representatives of many nations met in San Francisco to found a new organization, the United Nations. They hoped that it would prevent future wars and the kinds of human rights violations perpetrated by the Nazis which had shocked the conscience of the world. All members therefore pledged themselves "to take joint and separate action in cooperation with the Organization for the achievement of a number of purposes which the United Nations shall promote."[14] One of the most important of the purposes identified was that of securing human rights. Human rights were regarded as so important that they not only were mentioned prominently in the Preamble to the Charter for the new organization, but were singled out for attention in six different articles of the Charter, as well. Even so, some delegates to the United Nations Conference wanted to do more than endorse human rights in general terms. They wanted to write an international bill of rights which would become part of the Charter. No specific bill of rights was included in the Charter, however, because the majority of delegates believed it required greater and more detailed consideration than they could give to it at the time. But the delegates did name a Commission on Human Rights, and they instructed that Commission to undertake the task of writing a bill of rights immediately.

7. What Is the Universal Declaration of Human Rights, and Why Is It of Significance?

After the San Francisco meeting during which the United Nations was born in 1945, the Commission on Human Rights began its work. The first and most important task of that Commission was to write a Universal Declaration of Human Rights which was intended to be "a common standard of achievement for all peoples and all nations."

The Declaration consists of 30 Articles which enumerate civil, political, economic, social, and cultural rights, and fundamental freedoms to which every human being is entitled. It, therefore, is kind of a yardstick, providing the criteria by which respect for human rights can be measured worldwide.

On December 10, 1948, the Universal Declaration of Human Rights was adopted by the General Assembly of the United Nations by a vote of 48 to 0, with 8 absentions and two absences. This adoption was final; neither signature nor ratification was necessary.

Like most General Assembly resolutions, the Universal Declaration

---

[14]The United Nations Charter, *passim.*

is not legally binding. Even so, it has become a very significant document. Its effects have been felt and they can be observed in at least three important areas:

(1) Ever since its adoption, the Declaration has been used as a standard of conduct and as a basis for appeals urging governments to observe human rights.

(2) Global and regional treaties have been prepared which have transformed the Universal Declaration into international conventional law.

(3) The constitutions, laws, and court decisions of many nations and international bodies now show the marked influence of the Universal Declaration.[15]

The Declaration is a highly significant document because it represents the consensus of the international community. It defines more specifically the rights and freedoms referred to in the United Nations Charter. It expresses the "common understanding of the peoples of the world concerning the inalienable rights of all members of the human family and constitutes an obligation for the members of the international community."[16]

8. What Rights — "Old" and "New" — Does the Universal Declaration Proclaim?

The Universal Declaration of Human Rights is a unique document in the annals of world history, because, in its 30 articles, the Declaration both affirms "old" rights and proclaims "new" ones.

Traditional or "classical" civil and political rights contained in various constitutional and fundamental laws of the eighteenth and nineteenth centuries sometimes are referred to as "old" rights, because they long have been asserted. Articles 5, 7, and 10 in the Universal Declaration of Human Rights are examples of "old" or classical rights. Those Articles declare:

- No one shall be subjected to torture or to cruel, inhuman, or degrading treatment or punishment.
- All are equal before the law and are entitled without any discrimination to equal protection of the law.
- Everyone is entitled in full equality to a fair and public hearing by an independent and impartial tribunal, in the determination of his rights and obligations and of any criminal charge against him.

The Declaration also asserts "new" rights, those of an economic, social or cultural nature. The constitutions of many countries, includ-

---

[15]Dennis B. Driscoll, "The Development of Human Rights Into International Law," in *The Human Rights Reader*, edited by Walter Laqueur and Barry Rubin (New York: New American Library, 1979), pp. 45–46.

[16]Proclamation of Tehran, paragraph 2, adopted at the International Conference on Human Rights, 13 May 1968.

ing the United States, do not mention "new rights" specifically. New rights are implied in "general welfare" clauses, and they have been recognized through the passage of laws or by court decisions. The Universal Declaration of Human Rights, in contrast, makes economic, social, and cultural rights explicit. Articles 24, 26, and 27, for example, declare:

- Everyone has the right to rest and leisure, including reasonable limitation of working hours and periodic holidays with pay.
- Everyone has the right to education. Education shall be free, at least in the elementary and fundamental stages.
- Everyone has the right freely to participate in the cultural life of the community, to enjoy the arts and to share in scientific advancement and its benefits.
- Everyone has the right to the protection of the moral and material interests resulting from any scientific, literary, or artistic production of which he is the author.

The Universal Declaration not only has reaffirmed those civil and political rights long regarded as fundamental to human freedom, it has enunciated economic, social, and cultural rights more recently recognized as essential to human dignity.

9. What Is the International Bill of Rights?

The International Bill of Rights is not a single document. Instead, it is the name given to a series of documents which, taken together, form the foundation upon which "the house of human rights" has continued to be built by the international community.

The first step toward the formulation of the International Bill of Rights was taken with the acceptance of the United Nations Charter. All nations which have signed the Charter are bound by its provisions, because it is a treaty which obligates them to promote respect for and observance of human rights.

The second and perhaps the most important step in the formulation of the International Bill of Rights was taken with the proclamation of the Universal Declaration of Human Rights in 1948. The Declaration remains the most complete statement of international human rights.

The third step in the formulation of the International Bill of Rights was taken in 1966. In that year, the General Assembly of the United Nations adopted two Covenants—the Covenant on Economic, Social and Cultural Rights, and the Covenant on Civil and Political Rights.[17] Those Covenants were designed to transform the principles proclaimed in the Universal Declaration into binding treaty obligations.

---

[17]For the text of these instruments and further explanation of them, see Thomas Buergenthal and Judith V. Torney, *International Human Rights and International Education* (Washington, D.C.: U.S. National Commission for UNESCO, 1976).

The Covenants also were designed to establish international machinery to supervise and enforce the application of guaranteed rights. Although the Covenants were adopted in 1966, they did not go into effect until 1976, when a sufficient number of states had become parties to them. Since the Covenants went into effect, still more states have ratified them. As of September 1, 1981, sixty-six states had become parties to the Covenant on Economic, Social and Cultural Rights, and sixty-eight states had ratified the Covenant on Civil and Political Rights.

In the same year in which the UN General Assembly adopted the Covenants, it also accepted the Optional Protocol to the Covenant on Civil and Political Rights. The Protocol provides a means whereby individuals who feel that their own governments have violated their human rights may appeal to the Commission on Human Rights of the United Nations. If the aggrieved individual cannot appear in person, another may represent him or her. The right of appeal, however, is restricted to citizens of those countries which have ratified the Optional Protocol. As of September 1, 1981, twenty-five nations had done so.

The International Bill of Rights today, therefore, consists of the following documents:

- The United Nations Charter
- The Universal Declaration of Human Rights
- The Covenant on Civil and Political Rights
- The Covenant on Economic, Social and Cultural Rights
- The Optional Protocol to the Covenant on Civil and Political Rights

10. What Processes and Procedures Does the United Nations Have for Dealing with Human Rights Violations?

Ultimately, the international protection of human rights depends upon the existence of efficient and fair processes and procedures for dealing with human rights violations. To date, no such international system exists, even though the United Nations has made human rights a concern of many of its subdivisions. Among them are:

Economic and Social Council (ECOSCOC)
Commission on Human Rights
Sub-Commission on Prevention of Discrimination
     and Protection of Minorities
Commission on the Status of Women
Trusteeship Council
Office of the UN High Commission for Refugees (UNHCR)
International Labor Organization (ILO)
United Nations Educational, Scientific and Cultural Organization
(UNESCO)

Most of the agencies listed above are concerned in the main with the formation of international public policy on human rights. Three of those subdivisions, however, do assume responsibilities for monitoring human rights violations. The Commission on Human Rights and the Sub-Commission on Prevention of Discrimination and Protection of Minorities are empowered to investigate situations which reveal "a consistent pattern of violations of human rights." In the past, they have investigated human rights violations in South Africa, Chile, Cyprus, and occupied territories of the Middle East. They have been frustrated, however, in attempts to investigate alleged violations in some other parts of the world.

The Human Rights Committee consists of 18 independent experts nominated by their governments, but who are not representatives of their governments. By asking experts to serve in independent capacities, it is hoped that the dangers of politicization of the Committee can be minimized.

The Human Rights Committee receives and examines reports about progress being made in meeting the standards set forth in the Covenants. It is empowered to receive complaints from one country that another country is not meeting its obligations under the Covenants. The Committee also can act on complaints by individuals, provided that their governments are signatories to the Optional Protocol. Complaints are considered in private meetings. The Committee then makes its comments to the individual and to the state concerned.

It is easy enough to fault the United Nations and its agencies by pointing out that they lack "real" power to enforce their findings, or that they have been selective in expressing their indignation about human rights violations. Nonetheless, the fact that some processes and procedures do exist for the investigation of human rights violations is a first and significant step.

11. What Regional Organizations Are Concerned with the Protection of Human Rights?

At present there are two regional organizations which have processes and procedures for dealing with human rights violations. A third and perhaps a fourth regional organization are under consideration.

The most effective and longest-lived regional organization is in Western Europe. After World War II, nations which were part of the Council of Europe met to draft the European Convention for the Protection of Human Rights and Fundamental Freedoms. Today 20 of the 21 members of that Council have ratified the Convention. It not only obligates members to respect the human rights enumerated in the Universal Declaration, but the Convention also provides enforcement machinery. The European Human Rights Commission, which is one part of that machinery, holds confidential hearings and has three distinct functions:

(1)   To establish the facts in cases brought by one member state against another or by individuals against states.
(2)   To try to get the contending parties to reach fair and friendly settlements.
(3)   To write a report stating the Commission's opinion on questions of violation, if it cannot get the parties to agree to a settlement.

While the Commission cannot make a decision in cases of human rights violations, the European Court of Human Rights can. So, too, can the Committee of Foreign Ministers. The Court and the Committee are also part of the enforcement machinery provided for by the Convention. Whichever body makes the decision, the governments have agreed to accept it as binding.

The second functioning regional organization is the Organization of American States (OAS), which includes all of the states of the Western Hemisphere, except Canada, Cuba, and Guyana. The OAS took its first step toward the protection of human rights in 1948 by drawing up An American Declaration on the Rights and Duties of Man. That Declaration was unanimously adopted. In 1959, an Inter-American Commission on Human Rights was established. Then, ten years later, in 1969, the American Convention of Human Rights was drafted. It entered into force in September, 1978, when the required eleven member states had ratified the Convention. The United States has signed, but not yet ratified, the American Convention.

In many respects, the American Convention is similar to the European Convention. It provides for an Inter-American Commission on Human Rights which conducts fact-finding missions, hears witnesses, and consults with the governments concerned. The American Convention also provides for an Inter-American Court of Human Rights, which has been established in Costa Rica.

Although regional systems are not yet operative in Africa and the Middle East, there is evidence of interest in establishing them.

12. What Are NGOs and How Do They Work for Human Rights?

NGOs are nongovernmental organizations, and there are thousands of them at work for the protection and promotion of human rights.[18] The four best-known are:

(1)   The International Committee of the Red Cross, which was established in Switzerland in 1863. Its primary concern has been to see

---

[18]For further information, see *The Human Rights Handbook: A Guide to British and American International Human Rights Organizations*, compiled by Marguerite Garling for the Writers and Scholars International Trust (New York: Facts on File, 1979). See, also, *Encyclopedia of Associations*, 16th ed., 1982, available in most reference libraries.

that the laws of warfare are observed and that minimum standards obtained in the treatment of prisoners of war. More recently, the Red Cross has been concerned with the rights of political prisoners, as well.

(2)   The International League for Human Rights, which formerly was known as the International League for Human Rights of Man. Founded in New York in 1942, this organization is concerned primarily with the drafting of human rights standards within the United Nations.

(3)   The International Commission of Jurists. This group, composed of no more than 40 eminent jurists, is dedicated to the support and advancement of the rule of law worldwide.

(4)   Amnesty International. Founded in London in 1961, Amnesty International now has sections in more than 30 countries, including the United States. It is the strongest organized international pressure group for the respect of human rights. Amnesty International, the recipient of the 1977 Nobel Prize for Peace, works impartially for the release of prisoners of conscience, especially those men and women detained anywhere for their conscientiously held beliefs, color, ethnic origin, sex, religion, or language, provided they have neither used nor advocated violence. Amnesty International opposes torture and the death penalty without reservation. It seeks fair and prompt trials for all political prisoners, and it monitors those trials whenever possible.

The number of NGOs has multiplied dramatically in recent years. One scholar estimated that there were about 4,000 of them in 1974 which were concerned with the promotion of human rights in one way or another.[19]

NGOs employ a variety of strategies. They lobby before the United Nations and regional organizations. They conduct investigations, make reports, and issue public statements designed to influence public opinion. In the United States, NGOs, sometimes working together, have continued to urge ratification of various human rights treaties and the passage of human rights legislation.

Some NGOs have been criticized for their lack of objectivity and reliability, but there is no disputing the fact that they have served their purpose of keeping human rights high on the world's agenda, and they have provided a means whereby individuals interested in human rights can volunteer their services.

[19]James Frederick Green, "NGO's," in *Human Rights and World Order*, edited by Abdul Aziz Said (New York: Praeger Publishers, 1978), p. 96.

13. Why Do the Human Rights of Children, Women, and Ethnic Minorities Deserve Special Attention?

History is replete with examples of disregard for the human rights of children, women, and ethnic minorities. These three groups of human beings have been especially vulnerable to violations, and they too often have been excluded from participating in those bodies before which they might have presented their cases. For that reason, special efforts now are being made on their behalf.

The United Nations has endeavored to help children in a number of ways. One way is by focusing attention on the special needs of children. The General Assembly did that by adopting unanimously in 1959 a Declaration of the Rights of the Child. That Declaration, which the United Nations continues to publicize, insists that children are entitled to the best that society has to offer. It enjoins parents, individuals, voluntary organizations, local authorities, and States to recognize their duties toward children and to afford them the special protections to which they are entitled. Another way in which the United Nations helps children is through the United Nations Children's Fund (UNICEF). UNICEF is the oldest of the United Nations agencies, and it provides direct assistance to children when and where it is most needed. Still another way in which concern for children has been shown is in the observance of 1979 as the International Year of the Child.

The United Nations also has attempted in a variety of ways to promote the rights of women. It has adopted a number of Conventions designed to secure for women rights commensurate with those enjoyed by men. It has established the United Nations Commission on the Status of Women. That Commission meets every other year to examine what progress toward equality women are making throughout the world and to recommend further actions which need to be taken.

A major step in acknowledging the needs of ethnic minorities was taken when the United Nations drew up the International Convention on the Elimination of All Forms of Racial Discrimination. That treaty entered into force in 1969. It now has been ratified by 97 States, and it represents the most comprehensive United Nations statement regarding discrimination based on race, color, or ethnic origin. Under provisions of the Convention, a special Committee on the Elimination of Racial Discrimination was established. The Committee meets regularly to hear complaints and to monitor governmental compliance.

While the efforts which have been made thus far are to be applauded, it is obvious that much more needs to be done to safeguard and to enhance the human rights of children, women, and ethnic minorities.

14. Rights and Duties: Why Does One Involve the Other?

People sometimes are heard to complain that there is too much emphasis on rights and too little on duties. Properly understood, however, rights do not exist apart from duties; rights and duties really are two sides of the same coin. Article 29 of the Universal Declaration of Human Rights makes that very clear. It asserts that "Everyone has duties to the community in which alone the free and full development of his personality is possible." In other words, rights and duties are intertwined; they are concepts which are interconnected. No one, perhaps, has explained the interconnection between rights and duties more clearly than the late internationally renowned scholar Charles Frankel. He said:

In normal legal terms, a *right* exists when, under the law, there is a corresponding *duty*. If Jones, for example, has a right to privacy in his home, this means that everyone not in his immediate family has a *duty* to keep out, unless Jones permits entry, or a court-ordered warrant is presented. Similarly, if an individual claims a *moral right*, he is normally taken to be saying that under the rules of a recognized moral code, certain people or members of society at large, have a definite *duty* toward him. In everyday parlance, then, the word *rights* says something more than it would be a good policy for people to behave in certain ways, or that it is desirable that they adjust their conduct and seek certain goals. To claim a *right* is to say that people MUST behave in a prescribed manner, and that the existence of a *right* is, in and by itself, the sufficient reason why they must. Only strong and recognized reasons can exempt them from this duty.[20]

15. Why Is Informed World Opinion Regarding Human Rights Important?

The importance of informed world opinion about human rights can scarcely be overemphasized. As one internationally recognized jurist reminds us:

This international human rights code. . . is in existence today only because of the pressure of public opinion generated by mankind's shared commitment to the protection of human rights in all parts of the world. But denials of human rights do not end just because there are laws prohibiting them. Many governments continue to commit violations of basic human rights.[21]

Because these serious violations continue, it is extremely important that there be a deep-seated, broadly based commitment to learning and teaching about human rights. A recent meeting of educators from

---

[20]Charles Frankel, *Human Rights and Foreign Policy* (New York: The Foreign Policy Association, Headline Series 241, October, 1978), p. 37.

[21]Thomas Buergenthal, "A Challenge for the Universities," *The UNESCO Courier* (October, 1978), p. 26.

various parts of the world concluded with the hope that every child in the world would become as familiar with the Universal Declaration of Human Rights as with the human rights provisions of the constitutions of their own nations or states.

A long road lies ahead, but it must be traversed, if the present state of heightened awareness of human rights is to be turned into the kind of sustained and informed world opinion essential for their protection and implementation.

1920s . . . the migrants arrive and cast their ballots. Jacob Lawrence. 1917- . USA.
Gouache, 1974. Courtesy Terry Dintenfass Galleries, New York.

UNIVERSAL DECLARATION OF HUMAN RIGHTS

The right to take part in the government

Article 21.   (1) Everyone has the right to take part in the government of his country, directly or through freely chosen representatives.

(3) The will of the people shall be the basis of . . . government; this will shall be expressed in periodic . . . elections which shall be by universal and equal suffrage . . . .

Article 7.   All are equal before the law and are entitled without any discrimination to equal protection of the law. All are entitled to equal protection against any discrimination in violation of this Declaration and against any incitement to such discrimination.

Chapter 2

INTERNATIONAL HUMAN RIGHTS AND CIVIC EDUCATION

R. Freeman Butts

Three major drives are competing to reshape the social studies in American schools. Despite their common interest in social studies, these efforts to redirect the curriculum are often carried out independently of one another. There has been too little effort to interweave the three and too little recognition of their natural affinity. Indeed, they are often disparate, and sometimes even antagonistic, in their impacts or pressures upon the schools.

Three Competing Movements in the Social Studies

The first of these movements is international or global education, a variety of efforts to internationalize the perspectives of American citizens in light of the realities of the global interdependence of nation states and the need for a peaceful and secure world community. This interest in international education is underway in other nations of the world, as well as in the United States. For example, in 1974 UNESCO approved a *Recommendation Concerning Education for International Understanding, Co-operation and Peace and Education Relating to Human Rights and Fundamental Freedoms*, and many nations in all areas of the world are taking action to implement it.

The second drive is the pluralistic effort to enhance the distinctive cultural traditions of the different ethnic and racial groups that comprise American society. The call for public schools to embrace a philosophy of cultural pluralism has spread rapidly during the past decade. The most visible signs in the schools have been the introduction of bilingual and multicultural studies into the curriculum. The Ethnic Heritage Studies Act, the Bilingual Education Act, and the Teacher Corps Act are examples; and many professional teachers' associations, including the National Council for the Social Studies,

23

have embraced multicultural education with enthusiasm. The "Curriculum Guidelines for Multiethnic Education" (1976) greatly influenced the revised NCSS "Curriculum Guidelines of 1979" (*Social Education*, April 1979).

The third development is a remarkable revival of interest in citizenship education in an effort to generate greater social and civic cohesion and commitment to the historic democratic political values basic to a common American citizenship. The U.S. Office of Education sponsored national and regional conferences through its Citizenship Education staff. A National Task Force on Citizenship Education was sponsored by the Kettering and Danforth Foundations. The Council of Chief State School Officers formed a special committee on this subject, as well as on international education. Perhaps most significantly, the American Bar Association has stimulated widespread projects through its Special Committee on Youth Education for Citizenship. All of these efforts resulted in an amendment to the Elementary and Secondary Education Act, authorizing funds for the Law-Related Education Act of 1978.

Clearly, these three movements all directly address the national interest; all three aim to improve our capacities for living humanely and justly with one another; all three aim to improve our understanding of intercultural conflict and our ability to resolve it.

Unfortunately, too often in the past, these movements have conceived their roles and goals narrowly and provincially. Civic education at its worst has been guilty of having stressed chauvinism, an unreasoning ethnocentric patriotism that has served America ill in the eyes of much of the world. "Citizenship Education" has often meant a conformist Americanization of immigrant and ethnic groups. Multicultural studies frequently have stressed the diversities and differences of segmented ethnic groups while neglecting concern for building a common, viable political community. And international studies have stressed understanding *other* peoples and their cultures with little concern for the international character of developments within the American political community.

One of the effects of these narrow conceptions has been the emergence of these movements virtually as special interests lobbying in the schools, working at cross purposes, each trying to make its separate claim on teachers and school resources. The schools are often caught in the middle, as they attempt with one hand to develop new bilingual, multicultural, and ethnic heritage studies, and with the other to develop new civic or international education programs. Scarce resources are diluted, the commonality of purpose shared by the special interests is obscured, opportunities for mutual assistance and cooperative efforts are lost, and, as administrators unsuccessfully attempt to juggle the several political elements, programs suffer—or worse—are dropped.

The Study of International Human Rights: A Link

I strongly urge social studies educators to increase the extent to which education for civic cohesion and education for cultural pluralism are linked together and interwoven with education for global interdependence. I believe that this can be done especially well through emphasis upon international human rights. In its concern for strengthening the American polity, citizenship education can no longer ignore the rest of the world; in its concern for recognizing the necessities of an emerging world community, international education can no longer ignore the health and vitality of the American political community. Education for interdependence means that basic civic literacy for American citizenship must include a reasoned awareness and understanding of:

- varying ways of life in other cultures
- the emerging world economic and political system
- the role of international organizations in international cooperation
- the intimate ways in which global problems impinge upon American communities, large and small.

American political leaders must decide basic questions of foreign policy and determine America's role in the world. American citizens, in turn, must evaluate their political leaders and their policies on the basis of these leaders' judgments. For that reason, the effectiveness of American foreign policy can be no better than the quality of the decisions Americans make about their leaders. And the quality of those decisions can surely be improved by an enriched civic education curriculum that pays special attention to the treatment of human rights in the various nations of the world. It is apparent to almost everyone that in recent years a startlingly large proportion of American citizens has lost confidence in the integrity, authority, and efficacy of public persons and governmental institutions. It is equally apparent that a large proportion of youth believes that our institutions do not practice the democratic values that the schools teach. It is significant that the two precipitating and reinforcing events for these trends were the Vietnam War and the Watergate affair, one an international and the other a domestic event. Insofar as education can help to reverse these trends of public attitude, it must conjoin its efforts for a revitalized citizenship education and a revitalized international education. The new civic literacy must embrace both. Moreover, the historic pluralism of American society is a striking example not only of the international comings and goings of millions of people across the continents and the seas, but of successes of the United States in building a genuinely cohesive, as well as pluralistic democratic society, despite persistent racism, nativism, segregation, discrimination, and inequality.

Building the Sense of a Just Civic Community

While the threefold stress on civic community in the United States, on cultural pluralism, and on the need for world community is of concern to teachers, I believe that they should pay particular attention to building the sense of a just civic community, which is essential for the maintenance and improvement of a healthy democratic American polity, serving well the values of cultural pluralism at home and global interdependence abroad.

My principal argument, then, is that these three major drives in social studies are naturally and rightly interdependent; that historical separations of these movements are essentially artificial and constitute a distortion of the logic which binds them together; that reasoned awareness of and respect for disparate cultures is increasingly necessary in a world of international conflict; that international security and justice are inseparably tied to the maintenance of an intelligent, informed citizenry; and that an intelligent citizenry is necessary to the maintenance of a society free of intolerance, racism, sexism, and ethnocentric behavior. These several impulses should be unified if the nation's interests in freedom, equality, justice, and the public good are to be served. Teaching and learning in the social studies have historically had a large part to play in these sets of values, but they have seldom been brought together in a coherent program of studies.

The theme of international human rights can be especially useful in showing how a foundation of trust in the political system can be strengthened in those countries where human rights are respected and weakened where human rights are ignored or violated. Learning about internationally recognized human rights, as well as about human rights violations, can in turn help students to understand the constitutional social contract and Bill of Rights in the United States and their parallels and variations in other societies.

Great strides have been made in recent years in developing new and exciting curriculum materials in civic education, in multicultural education, and in global education. I hope that now we can experiment with still newer materials that will consciously introduce pluralistic ideas and values into citizenship programs, and introduce international perspectives into both. I believe that the theme of international human rights is one of the most promising means for achieving these purposes.

In a recently published book, [1] I proposed a scheme of "democratic civic values" which stresses both the cohesive ideas and beliefs of our common political community and the distinctive pluralistic values of

---

[1] R. Freeman Butts, *The Revival of Civic Learning* (Bloomington, Ind.: Phi Delta Kappa Educational Foundation, 1980).

the various ethnic, religious, and racial groups in American society. I argued that the fundamental ideas, concepts, and civic values upon which our constitutional order is built should be the core of sustained study and searching criticism throughout the school years from kindergarten through high school and the years of liberal arts education and teacher education. I believe that the education profession, and especially those in social studies, should be trying much more rigorously and vigorously to become knowledgeable about the substantive concepts and ideas that form the common core of American citizenship.

To this end, I have proposed a set of ten value concepts—a decalogue, if you please—that I believe should be used as an intellectual framework in designing civic education programs for schools and colleges. I make no claim about their originality, but I think the conceptual scheme is somewhat unique. I have classified the ten value concepts into two general types: those that seem primarily to promote desirable cohesive and unifying elements in a democratic political community, and those that primarily promote desirable pluralistic and individualistic elements in a democratic political community. There is a continuing tension, and sometimes overt conflict, between the values of *Unum* and the values of *Pluribus;* but I believe that civic education must, like American democracy itself, try to balance, honor, and promote both. (See accompanying chart on p. 28.)

International Human Rights: A Basic Civic Value

My inclusion of "international human rights" as one of the basic civic values for study in programs of civic education provides an especially appropriate link with pluralistic and global themes in social studies. There obviously are other ways in which the idea of national citizenship may take into account the vast changes in the world situation which have burst upon our consciousness since the end of World War II. Increasingly popular terms to define the set of phenomena which began with the term "One World" in the 1940s are now "global interdependence," or simply "globalization." But these terms do not convey as well as "human rights" the notion that individuals are not to be discriminated against on the basis of their racial, national, cultural, ethnic, or gender differences. Discrimination is not, as American students may believe, a problem only in this country. International human rights documents and procedures attempt, at least partially, to correct or ameliorate discrimination by giving individuals means of protest and remedy when their distinctive cultural or ethnic values are attacked. Such study provides a link between the civic, the international, and the pluralistic values.

A DECALOGUE OF DEMOCRATIC CIVIC VALUES*

(with apologies to Moses and Aristotle)

Corrupted Forms	True Forms of Unum	True Forms of Pluribus	Corrupted Forms
"Law and order"	Justice	Freedom	Anarchy
Enforced sameness and conformity	Equality	Diversity	Unstable pluralism
Authoritarianism	Authority	Privacy	Privatism
"Majoritarianism"	Participation	Due Process	"Soft on criminals"
Chauvinism	Personal Obligation for the Public Good	International Human Rights	"Cultural imperialism"

Cosmopolitan Civism   Stable Pluralism

Pluralistic Civism

---

*R. Freeman Butts, *The Revival of Civic Learning* (Bloomington, Indiana: Phi Delta Kappa Foundation, 1980), p. 128.

Achieving Global Perspective on Rights

The link between civic and global themes can be stressed as students are made aware of which of their rights as American citizens are often protected in other countries and in international documents. One of the ways to overcome nativist chauvinism is for students to achieve a global or international perspective on rights and to acquire the awareness that many persons in other countries care about their rights and seek to protect them very much as we do in the United States.

An enormous amount of new educational material is being developed to make students aware of the many ways in which the earth has shrunk and the ways that events in one part of the world almost immediately have an impact upon conditions in other parts of the earth. The effect that raising oil prices or withholding oil production in the Middle East has on the corporate and individual lives of people all over the world is only one of the latest and most obvious examples. Similar interdependence can, of course, be pointed out in the fields of technology, space exploration, travel, communication, multinational organizations, political blocs, cultural styles, pop music, mass media, and on and on. The immensity of the problems and the prospective overloading of the curriculum with global teaching materials have led various groups to try to be somewhat selective in their approach.

The Mid-America Program in Bloomington, Indiana, and the Mershon Center at the Ohio State University stress ways in which the children of local communities in states like Indiana or Ohio can become aware of specific ways in which they themselves and their community are linked with what happens halfway around the world. The Center for Global Perspectives concentrates on four concepts (interdependence, conflict, communication, and change) as basic tools by which children and youth from kindergarten to grade 12 can organize knowledge and think about their relations to the interdependent world.

Whatever the principle of selection may be, it seems to me that the value context for a basic international ingredient in civic education is now more urgent than ever before. The world situation and the educational context changed during the 20 years from 1955 to 1975. In the 1950s and 1960s, a great motivation was to get American education to include more factual knowledge about other peoples of the world (largely through language and area studies impelled by the National Defense Education Act of 1958) and more factual knowledge about international relations, world affairs, and contemporary issues as a subdivision of political science. Comparative studies and foreign student exchange programs were also highlighted. The International Education Act of 1966 was supposed to internationalize the curriculum of

American schools and colleges and provide an academically solid and realistic education in world affairs for all Americans. However, it did not get off the ground, despite its passage by Congress at the insistence of Lyndon Johnson. One of the great ironies of the period was that international education became a casualty of Lyndon Johnson's international policies. While the ideas of global interdependence and a just world order were undoubtedly present in the 1960s, they were not the most visible concepts. "International understanding" and education for "development" or "modernization" were much more common terms. Now, the problems and issues for possible study are so vast and varied that some principle of selection is necessary, if civic education and international education are to support and complement one another.

While I would hope for a stronger linkage between citizenship education and international education, I do not believe that *all* of global or international studies should be subsumed under the rubric of citizenship education. Nor can all of civic education be assigned to global studies. There is simply too much on each side. I believe that global studies should be given much greater attention throughout the total school curriculum, but I believe that some principle of selection should be operating in order to bring an essential global perspective into the scope of civic education. I would argue that the requirements of American citizenship in the world today mean that civic education should select from the almost infinite masses of information those elements of world studies that focus upon international human rights and illuminate the other nine concepts in my decalogue of value claims. Discussions of international human rights necessarily involve questions of justice, freedom, equality, diversity, authority, privacy, due process, and participation, as these values are honored or violated in various nations, including the United States, and in the relations among nations.

Examples of the interplay between cohesive civic values and diversifying pluralistic values are especially pertinent in the realm of human rights. They can come from the denials of freedom, as in ethnic persecution culminating in the Holocaust of Hitler's Germany, or the devastation resulting from arbitrary rule in Amin's Uganda. They can come from achievements for human rights in Rhodesia's struggle to become Zimbabwe, or Nigeria's efforts to establish a constitutional regime after civil war and military rule. They can come from study of dissidents seeking freedom in Iran, China, Cuba, the Soviet Union, or military dictatorships in Latin Ameria. They can be illustrated by the Polish workers who claimed political rights for religious expression by the church and for physical freedom for political prisoners as well as the rights of trade unions to run their own affairs. And closer to home, they can be illustrated by the problems for human rights raised by the influx of Cubans and Haitians to Florida, and Mexicans, Vietnamese, and Koreans to Los Angeles. Historic problems of immigration, nativism, Americanization, segregation, and integration are all revived in contemporary confrontations over international as well as domestic human rights.

The Bicentennial of the U.S. Constitution and Human Rights

As we approach the bicentennial of the framing of the U.S. Constitution in 1787 and the adoption of the Bill of Rights in 1791, civic educators are being urged to reexamine the basic ideas and values of the American democratic civic community. I heartily approve of this move. I also would urge that a complementary study of some of the basic documents that set forth contemporary statements of international human rights should be undertaken to show their relationships to American ideals. Such documents include the United Nations Universal Declaration of Human Rights of 1948; the International Covenant on Economic, Social and Cultural Rights of 1966; the International Covenant on Civic and Political Rights of 1966; and a UNESCO statement headed by the formidable title "Recommendation Concerning Education for International Understanding, Co-operation and Peace and Education Relating to Human Rights and Fundamental Freedoms." The documents themselves often make laborious reading, for the diplomatic language can be difficult; however, careful selection of concepts and examples from history and from contemporary affairs could enable students to make illuminating comparisons and to see the United States as one participant in a world system. The twofold aim is that of considering how to improve the American political system as well as of considering how the United States could play a more constructive and humanitarian role in the world.

This interrelationship of the political health and vitality of the United States itself and the state of the world at large is further illustrated by the concerns of the recent President's Commission on Foreign Languages and International Studies. The Commission quickly and clearly recognized that pluralism in the United States should be viewed in relation to divergences and differences on the international scene. The prominence of the multicultural emphasis in the deliberations and report of the Commission attests to the success of the pluralist movements in advancing their cause in recent years. I believe that this is a sound and desirable recognition of the interconnection of the international and the pluralist concerns. However, I do not find that the Commission recognized so clearly that both of those approaches should be related to the revival of an American civic learning that must, more than ever before in our history, take account of the international as well as the pluralistic and cohesive values of our democratic political system.

Expanding Circles of Loyalty

A decade ago, Barbara Ward and René Dubos stated cogently and eloquently the ideal and the compatibility of expanding circles of loyalty from pluralistic groups to nation and to world community:

The emotional attachment to our prized diversity need not interfere with our attempts to develop the global state of mind which will generate a rational loyalty to the planet as a whole. As we enter the global phase of human evolution it becomes obvious that each man has two countries, his own and the planet Earth.

.   .   .

From family to clan, from clan to nation, from nation to federation—such enlargements of allegiances have occurred without wiping out the earlier loves. Today, in human society, we can perhaps hope to survive in all our prized diversity provided we can achieve an ultimate loyalty to our single, beautiful, and vulnerable planet Earth.[2]

This well states the goal of combining the values of stable pluralism with the values of a cosmopolitan civism. I use "stable pluralism" in Michael Kammen's sense that the freedoms and diversities and privacies that we should honor, respect, and encourage must be based upon a strong underpinning of political and psychological legitimacy which in turn arises from cohesive elements of civism.[3] I use "cosmopolitan civism" in John Higham's sense of America's historically generous, open, tolerant approach to difference rather than its narrow, bigoted, provincial demands for conformity;[4] and now, of course, "cosmopolitan" applies to human rights throughout the world itself.

So I argue for an international, multicultural, and civic education that recognizes the persisting tensions and yet seeks for a continuing balance between a cosmopolitan civism and a stable pluralism. The need for sustained study and search for such a balance between civism and pluralism is just as great in the liberal education of colleges and

---

[2]Barbara Ward and René Dubos, *Only One Earth: The Care and Maintenance of a Small Planet* (New York: North, 1972), pp. xviii and 220.

[3]Michael Kammen, *People of Paradox: An Inquiry Concerning the Origins of American Civilization* (New York: Vintage Books, 1973), p. 85.

[4]John Higham, *Strangers in the Land: Patterns of American Nativism, 1860–1925* (New York: Atheneum, 1974), p. 20.

universities, and especially in teacher education, as it is in elementary and secondary schools. A concerted revival of this kind of civic learning at all levels of the educational system could most appropriately take place during the decade that culminates with the two-hundredth anniversary of the framing and adoption of the United States Constitution and the development of the American version of a Bill of Human Rights.

Fishing. Soroseelutu Ashoona. 1941-   . Canada.
Stonecut litho, 1976. Collection of Ben Goldstein.

UNIVERSAL DECLARATION OF HUMAN RIGHTS

The family is entitled to protection

Article 16.   (1) Men and women of full age, without any limitation due to race, nationality or religion, have the right to marry and to found a family. They are entitled to equal rights as to marriage, during marriage and at its dissolution.

(3) The family is the natural and fundamental group unit of society and is entitled to protection by society and the State.

Chapter 3

SOCIALIZATION AND HUMAN RIGHTS RESEARCH: IMPLICATIONS FOR TEACHERS

Judith Torney-Purta

The effectiveness of human rights education depends on many things—student interest, teacher awareness and preparation, and adequacy of materials, to name only a few. The purpose of this chapter is to review existing research on what young people know and believe about human rights and about their place in a global context in order to improve the effectiveness of this education. There are four types of research which are especially relevant. The first is research on citizenship education—knowledge and attitudes in the areas of civil liberties, democratic values, and political rights. The second is research on international and global orientations, relating specifically to views of foreign nations and peoples and to awareness of the universal desire for human dignity and rights. The third is research in the area of social cognition, relating to children's concepts of social institutions, ability to take the perspective of others, and concepts of justice and equality. The fourth is research on classroom climate and student participation.

Using the information from these four areas of research, a series of questions will be addressed:

(1) What do young people know and believe about human rights and about their universality? What common misconceptions do they hold?

(2) What is known about the best sequence and the timing of instruction in human rights?

(3) Which methods seem most effective in human rights education? How do the informal curriculum and classroom climate affect human rights education?

Existing Knowledge and Beliefs About Human Rights and Their Universality

In addition to the legal and political history of the universal search for human rights (discussed in Chapter 1), there is also considerable empirical evidence that there are deeply held belief structures about the importance of respect for basic human rights.

One small study conducted recently with children aged nine through thirteen explored the extent to which there is consensus concerning the moral dimension of human rights.[1] Children were asked questions taken directly from the Universal Declaration of Human Rights: for example, "suppose that in another country it was decided that it was all right to put someone in prison for several years without going to court or having a trial. In that country they had no laws saying that people should have a trial before being put in jail. Would that be right?" Another question asked, "What if someone in another country was arrested, and the police thought that he was guilty, but the person wouldn't admit it. Would it be right if there were a law that said the police could beat the person to get him to admit to the crime or to get evidence?" In response to these questions (and others like them dealing with basic human rights—including the right not to be held in slavery), ninety to one hundred percent of American children said that no law enacted by a country could justify actions which violated rights in this way. This suggests that there may be a deeply held belief that human beings have certain rights by virtue of being human. Some of the young people commented spontaneously that a government which holds people in slavery, tortures them, or refuses them a trial "is not a good government" or "can't expect much respect from its people." It should also be noted that although they could express well thought-out comments about these provisions of the Universal Declaration of Human Rights, most children were unable to respond when asked for a definition of human rights.

In another study of beliefs and concepts, Gallatin[2] interviewed young people aged 11 to 18 from the United States, Great Britain, and the Federal Republic of Germany. Hers was primarily a study of conceptions of the domestic social and political order and of rights associated with it. Some of the findings relate to the issues of universality, however. Age group differences were far more impressive than differences between the nations. Gallatin concluded from the student interviews that a certain philosophy of rights was commonly accepted:

---

[1] J. Torney and P. Brice. "Children's Concepts of Human Rights and Social Cognition." Paper presented at the American Psychological Association, 1979.

[2] J. Gallatin. "The Conceptualization of Rights: Psychological Development and Cross National Perspectives." In R.P. Claude (Ed.), *Comparative Human Rights* (Baltimore: Johns Hopkins University Press, 1976).

Whatever their differences, these three nations share, at least in recent history, a common political philosophy which stipulates that the rulers serve the ruled and the government is obligated to furnish certain basic services for its citizens and grant them a set of inalienable rights.[3]

Another study dealt with university students in Hong Kong, France, and the United States.[4] Bloom found two separate dimensions to be common to all three cultures—"social principledness" (the ability to differentiate between a conventional and a personal standard of morality in making socio-political decisions) and "social humanness" (the tendency to give priority to the human implications of decisions).

The IEA survey of civic education in ten nations, in which more than thirty thousand young people aged 10, 14, and 17–20 were surveyed in 1971, included a number of items dealing with human rights.[5] When these items were factor-analyzed, a strong dimension emerged which included scales relating to discrimination on the basis of race and religion, beliefs concerning the equality of treatment of different social groups, issues of civil and political rights concerned with citizens' freedom to criticize the government, and the political rights of women. Scores on the scales measuring racial and religious discrimination indicated a high level of tolerance and relatively few differences between adolescent attitudes in nations as diverse as the Netherlands, the Federal Republic of Germany, Finland, Italy and the USA. In contrast, there were very large differences among countries and much less tolerance expressed on the scale measuring support for women's rights. (The fourteen-year-olds in the United States had lower scores on this scale than students in any of the other eight nations tested at that age level.) At least at the verbal level, there seems to be substantial support among adolescents in these nations for equality of treatment for racial and religious minorities. However, discrimination against women appears to be the most difficult area in which to achieve consensus about rights, even in Western societies.

A recent survey conducted by the Educational Testing Service and the Council on Learning included a number of items measuring attitudes toward human rights among college freshmen and seniors, as well as students in two-year colleges. Approximately one thousand freshmen were tested from a stratified sample drawn from throughout the United States. These data represent the attitudes of those who have recently left the secondary school and been admitted to higher education. Seventy-five to eighty percent of these students agreed with items such as the following: "Political freedom is a basic human right and no government should be permitted to abridge it"; and "no government

---

[3]Gallatin, *op. cit.*, p. 323.

[4]A.H. Bloom. "Two Dimensions of Moral Reasoning: Social Principledness and Social Humanism in Cross-cultural Perspective." *Journal of Social Psychology*, 101, 1977, pp. 29–44.

[5]J.V. Torney; A.N. Oppenheim; and R.F. Farnen. *Civic Education in Ten Countries: An Empirical Study* (New York: Wiley, 1975).

should deny access to basic education to any of its citizens." In contrast, less than twenty percent agreed with the following statement: "It is none of our business if other governments restrict the personal freedom of their citizens."[6] These same freshmen ranked "The Denial of Basic Human Rights" as fourth in importance out of ten global issues. To be more concrete, it was seen as less important than Malnutrition or Health and War or Armaments, but as more important than Overpopulation.

These freshmen were also asked to rate eight global problems on several scales, including whether they were "solvable or unsolvable," and whether they were "avoidable or unavoidable." The Denial of Basic Human Rights, Malnutrition or Health, and Environmental Pollution were the three problems which freshmen rated as the most solvable and avoidable. These ratings contrasted considerably with the rating for Inflation, for example.

This review of quite disparate sources of data leads to the conclusion that a very large proportion of children in the United States believe that a search for basic human rights is universal among human beings and that governments ought to respect these rights. This belief seems to persist through high school. Even college freshmen do not see human rights as a hopeless or intractable problem.

Although students believe that human rights ought to be universally respected, their level of information about this subject is not as high as one might wish. For example, only about forty percent of the 13- and 17-year-olds tested by the National Assessment of Educational Progress knew that the United Nations could take action against a member country which violated the human rights of those of different races.[7] In the ETS survey of college students, half of the items regarding human rights appeared in the list of items showing serious misconceptions on the part of students.[8] Only questions dealing with religious issues showed a higher proportion of misconceptions. About half the students knew that the United Nations promulgated the Universal Declaration of Human Rights following World War II. A substantial proportion of able students attributed it either to the League of Nations or to Amnesty International. More than three-quarters of the freshmen overestimated the number of human rights treaties which the United States had ratified. In a related area, a substantial number of students did not realize that apartheid involves the separation of races by law, not merely personal prejudice. One might argue that students should be expected to gain some of their knowledge of human rights from college courses and not expect the secondary school to teach everything. It

[6]T. Barrows. "Attitudes and Perceptions." In T. Barrows (Ed.), *What College Students Know About Their World* (New Rochelle, N.Y.: Change Magazine Press, 1981).

[7]National Assessment of Educational Progress. *Education for Citizenship: A Bicentennial Survey* (Denver: Educational Commission of the States, 1976).

[8]S.F. Klein and S.M. Ager. "Knowledge." In T. Barrows (Ed.), *op. cit.*

appears, however, that a substantial part of the discussion of world problems reported by college freshmen took place during their high school years. While eighty percent of freshmen reported that world issues had been discussed at least once a week in their high school classes, only slightly more than half reported such frequent discussion in college classes.

In addition to data about specific misconceptions regarding human rights, there is one further concern which is less firmly substantiated by data. An examination of curriculum material indicates that when the domestic political scene is presented, the stress is on consensus and agreement, even to the extent of denying the existence of conflicting opinions in American politics. In contrast, when presenting foreign cultures and international relations, the stress is placed on conflict, disagreement, and differences.[9] Although presentations of cultural relativism are an important part of the curriculum in social studies, it is unfortunate if children learn only about differences between themselves and those in other nations, and focus only on war and conflict.

Sequence and Timing in Human Rights Education

There are three principles for basing decisions about when and in what order various aspects of human rights education should be presented for optimal effectiveness: the primacy principle, the recency principle, and the plasticity principle.

The *primacy principle* is sometimes invoked to support the argument for early instruction. Since all learning is cumulative, the earlier an experience takes place in the child's life the more formative it is likely to be, it is argued. This principle relates directly to decisions about sequence in human rights education. There is a variety of ways in which topics may be ordered in the social studies. Textbook authors make their own decisions on the sequence of topics. Many history texts are ordered in chronological sequence. Posner and Strike[10] and Crabtree[11] have identified and studied a number of alternative sequences. If the primacy principle is operating, and concepts of rights are presented in a sequence which emphasizes American definitions first and international definitions later, if at all, many children will suffer from the misconception that only Americans enjoy the protection of their rights. This would not be the only area where sequence has been found to influence beliefs about the uniqueness of American political institu-

---

[9]J. Torney and T. Buergenthal. "Alternative Conceptions of Politically Relevant Socialization." Paper presented at Tutzing Conference on Political Socialization and Political Education, Tutzing, Federal Republic of Germany, 1977.

[10]G. Posner and K. Strike. "A Categorization Scheme for Principles of Sequencing Content." *Review of Educational Research*, 46, 1976, pp. 665–90.

[11]C. Crabtree. "Sequence and Transfer in Children's Learning of the Analytic Processes of Geography Inquiry." *Journal of Experimental Education*. 45, 1976, pp. 19–30.

tions. Data from the National Assessment indicate, for example, that a substantial proportion of students believe that the United States is the only country in the world with a written constitution. It is, after all, the constitution which is studied first, and, for many, it is the only such constitution studied. If one wished to give students the broadest understanding of human rights, one might present the Universal Declaration of Human Rights along with the United States Constitution and perhaps the constitutions of some other countries. In that sequence, the Universal Declaration would serve as the basis for organizing students' ideas about rights in a comparative framework.

The *recency principle* emphasizes the extent to which student learning is strongly influenced by recent events. Some of those who believe in this principle argue that education about national and international politics should be postponed until students are able to see direct links between their own welfare and politics and can actually engage in acts such as voting or campaigning—usually in late adolescence. Postponing all human rights education until late adolescence has not been demonstrated to be very effective, however.

Those who believe in the *plasticity principle* argue that middle childhood is the best time for human rights education. It appears to be a period in which a variety of important cognitive competencies have been achieved, but many concepts and attitudes are not yet rigid or fixed. There is considerable psychological research evidence supporting the plasticity principle and the importance of middle childhood. Selman[12] and Flavell,[13] who have conducted extensive studies of role taking and interpersonal perspective, both point to middle childhood as a time of especially rapid development.

Montemayor and Eisen asked young people, "who are you?" The response "a person" or "a human" was given by fewer than five percent of the 10-year-olds, but by a striking 80 percent of the 12-year-olds.[14] Less than half of the 14- and 17-year-olds gave that answer. Perhaps 12-year-olds are especially ready to adopt a "humankind" perspective. Melton studied children's comprehension of domestic rights and concluded, "most children have some idea of the nature of a right by the third grade. . . . It would appear that curricula about rights, particularly those belonging to children, could be meaningfully instituted as early as the third grade."[15] The problem of the child's concrete approach must be considered when instruction begins in the third or fourth grade, however. One must guard against the young

[12]R. Selman. "Social-cognitive Understanding: A Guide to Educational and Clinical Practice." In T. Lickona (Ed.), *Moral Development and Behavior* (New York: Holt, Rinehart & Winston, 1976).
[13]J.H. Flavell. "Role-taking and Communication Skills in Children." *Young Children*, 21, 1966, 164–77.
[14]R. Montemayor and M. Eisen. "The Development of Self-Conceptions from Childhood to Adolescence." *Developmental Psychology*, 13, 1977, pp. 314–19.
[15]G.B. Melton. "Children's Concepts of Their Rights." *Journal of Clinical Child Psychology*, 1980, pp. 186–190.

person's tendency to interpret "free" as meaning without payment, or "equal" as meaning numerically balanced, and the tendency to equate freedom with license to do whatever one pleases in ignorance of others' rights, or to equate economic freedom with greedy self-interest.[16]

A review of studies of perceptions of other persons and social situations also points to striking increases in the adequacy and complexity of children's perceptions in the years from about 7 to 12.[17] Perceptions of foreign people were studied by Lambert and Klineberg.[18] Three thousand children from three age levels (6, 10, and 14) from 11 different world areas were interviewed. The conclusions about American children were that those of about 10 years of age were particularly receptive to approaching and learning about foreign people; they did not limit their interest to those who were similar to themselves. By 14 years of age, these children appeared to be less open to viewing foreign people in a positive way. Other measures of stereotyping also increased between 10 and 14.

A study of American seventh- and twelfth-graders using a map-related technique found that the association of stereotypes with Africa and with Russia increased from the seventh to the twelfth grade.[19]

The increasing tendency to conform to peer group pressure is one possible reason for the decline in attitude plasticity in early to mid-adolescence. Most studies on this subject are conducted by observing young people in a controlled situation where they are required to make a perceptual judgment which may either conflict with or conform to a judgment made by peers. Strassberg and Wiggen found that conformity decreased with age between 8 and 11, but then increased up to age 13, the oldest age group tested.[20] Pasternack found that for boys, but not girls, conformity decreased from grade one through seven, then increased at grade eight.[21] Berndt found that conformity peaked at grade nine.[22] These results, along with similar ones found by Allen and Newston, indicate one possible explanation for the decline in attitude plasticity around 13 or 14.[23]

An area of psychological research which is quite closely connected to human rights is the study of belief in a just world and equity theory.

[16]D. Heater. *The Concepts, Attitudes and Skills Related to Human Rights* (Strasbourg, France; Council of Europe, in press).

[17]J. Torney. "The Elementary School Years as an Optimal Period for Learning about International Human Rights." In L. Falkenstein and C. Anderson (Eds.), *Daring to Dream: Law and the Humanities for Elementary Schools* (Chicago: American Bar Association, 1980).

[18]W. Lambert and O. Klineberg. *Children's Views of Foreign Peoples* (New York: Appleton-Century-Crofts, 1967).

[19]E. Hicks and B.K. Beyer. "Images of Africa." *Journal of Negro Education*, 39, 1970, pp. 155-70.

[20]D.S. Strassberg and E. Wiggen. "Conformity as a Function of Age in Pre-Adolescents." *Journal of Social Psychology*, 91, 1973, pp. 61–66.

[21]T.L. Pasternack. "Qualitative Differences in the Development of Yielding Behavior by Elementary School Children." *Psychological Reports*, 32, 1973, pp. 883–96.

[22]T. Berndt. "Developmental Changes in Conformity to Peers and Parents." *Developmental Psychology*, 15, 1979, pp. 608–16.

[23]V.L. Allen and D. Newston. "Development of Conformity and Independence." *Journal of Personality and Social Psychology*, 22, 1972, pp. 18–30.

Most of the research has been conducted with young adults, but a small number of studies of younger groups are intriguing. Lerner argues that the acquisition of ideas about justice is not merely a matter of absorbing social norms, but is a much more complicated process involving a certain amount of cognitive distortion.[24] Individuals have a stake in maintaining the belief that the world is just—that people get what they deserve. That "myth" allows the individual to justify his own enjoyment of positive outcomes and his own pursuit of self-interest. When confronted with a victim of blatant injustice, the individual will often either distort the view of the victim to emphasize the ways in which he or she really deserved to suffer (e.g., they brought it on themselves) or minimize the amount of suffering being experienced. Victims of human rights violations—hungry people in other nations, political prisoners, racial groups suffering discrimination—also are apt to be seen as somehow responsible for their fates. Individuals engage in these distortions, according to Lerner, because it allows them to believe that as long as they are "good people" they will not suffer a similar fate.

Under some conditions, however, individuals appear somewhat more ready to help rather than blame victims. These situations include times when the help is to be given to a single suffering victim, when the help is seen as only temporary, or when other factors allow the individual to help without violating the belief that people get what they deserve and that he or she need not fear becoming a victim.

Some research from England also is of interest in understanding attitudes toward victims of human rights violations. Studies of 14- and 15-year-old boys by Tajfel and his co-workers showed that the demands of equity were frequently ignored in order to give enhanced rewards to individuals who were perceived to be like oneself, in other words to be members of one's in-group.[25] Behavior which would be classified as inequity favoring the in-group was even stronger in this group in a study by Caddick.[26] One group performed a task under conditions which were clearly handicapping; the other group, which had achieved superiority by virtue of having been assigned an easier task, nevertheless engaged in inequity favoring the in-group in distributing resources at its command. These tasks have not yet been presented to younger children, but this research does give some indication of how notions of justice and equity may be shaped by in-group identification during adolescence. The period of middle childhood, therefore, appears to be the time when empathy for the victim is possible, because the desire to preserve in-group solidarity, characteristic of older adolescents, is not yet so strong.

[24]M.J. Lerner. *The Belief in a Just World* (New York: Plenum Publishing, 1980).

[25]H. Tajfel. "Experiments in Intergroup Discrimination." *Scientific American,* 223, 1970, pp. 96–102.

[26]B. Caddick, in L. Wheeler (Ed.), *Review of Personality and Social Psychology,* Vol. I (Beverly Hills: Sage, 1980).

In summary, there is some evidence for the operation of a plasticity principle. At about the age of seven, many children enter a period of rapid social-cognitive development and achieve at least rudimentary perspective-taking and concrete analytic skills. Although cognitive growth continues through adolescence, at about the age of 13 or 14 there appears to be a lessening of attitudinal plasticity and increased stereotyping. Attitudes become rigid, and they are used more frequently as a way of confirming peer group solidarity and excluding those who are different. The equitable treatment of others, especially those who may be victims of injustice or lack of opportunity, seems to be less important than maintaining the superior position of the in-group during adolescence. More research is necessary in all the areas relating to issues of timing and sequence, however.

Effective Instruction, Classroom Climate, and Human Rights Education

A recent review of the role of the school in political socialization has concluded that:

The school curriculum is found to be effective in transmitting knowledge but not in influencing attitudes. . . . Classroom climate and student participation in school activities, and the school organizational climate were main factors found related to student political attitudes.[27]

The IEA survey of civic education in a variety of countries found in almost all of them that scores on the scales measuring democratic values were highest among students whose classes included few printed drill exercises, little patriotic ritual, and large amounts of discussion where teachers allowed students to express their opinions and showed respect for them.[28] In one of the very few studies existing on human rights education, Kehoe compared two methods of dealing with the Universal Declaration.[29] In the first approach, teachers led students in discussion of cases related to the Universal Declaration of Human Rights to make pupils aware of its provisions and their application to specific cases of cultural practices which might be thought of as contraventions. Students were asked to consider what the consequences would be for society if everyone engaged in the behavior described. In a second approach, students did not stay in a single discussion group but moved from one area of the room to another. At each "learning station" an

---

[27]L. Ehman. "The American School in the Political Socialization Process." *Review of Educational Research*, 50, 1980, pp. 99–119.

[28]Torney, Oppenheim, and Farnen, *op. cit.*

[29]J. Kehoe. "An Examination of Alternative Approaches to Teaching the Universal Declaration of Human Rights." *International Journal of Political Education*, 3, 1980, pp. 193–204.

Article from the Universal Declaration was written on a large sheet of paper. A large envelope was attached to the paper containing newspaper stories describing contraventions of that Article. Groups of three or four students moved together to each station and discussed the Article as well as writing their reactions. A post-test evaluation of these students' knowledge of international law showed the second group to be superior.

There are a number of pieces of psychological research which lead to similar conclusions about the role of student-to-student interaction and involvement in planning and carrying out learning activities. Richter and Tjosvold compared elementary school students who were given the opportunity to choose topics and to plan major learning activities in their social studies classrooms with others who participated in teacher-planned activities.[30] Students who participated in discussion and planning were superior on a number of measures—more favorable attitudes toward school and social studies, more positive and less aggressive interactions with peers, more consistent behavior on tasks, and more effective learning. It is interesting to note the parallel these authors draw between this study and studies showing enhanced industrial production when workers are given responsibility for setting goals.

Furth's study of the way in which children's ideas of social institutions develop based on a Piagetian model points in a similar direction. Over the course of several interviews, he observed the process of children becoming convinced that old modes of thinking were inadequate and playfully experimenting with new modes.

The children on their own ask questions that reveal an internal conflict . . . they express discontent about their own opinions and correct themselves. . . . The social setting of these occasions is eminently suitable to developmental experience. The children are cooperating in conversation with another person who, although an adult, takes the children's viewpoints totally seriously in noncorrective and supportive fashion. They are like two peers working on a common problem.[31]

A recent study by Enright gave sixth-graders the responsibility for "tutoring" first-graders in social-cognitive skills of interpersonal relations and reciprocal perceptions of friendship.[32] After each tutoring session, the sixth-graders participated in groups in which they were encouraged to reflect actively upon these tutoring experiences—in particular upon perceptions of the need for social skills in various situations. A number of tests of reciprocity, social perception, and

---

[30]F.D. Richter and D. Tjosvold. "Effects of Student Participation in Classroom Decision Making on Attitudes, Peer Interaction, Motivation, and Learning." *Journal of Applied Psychology*, 65, 1980, pp. 74–80.

[31]H. Furth. *The World of Grown-Ups* (New York: Elsevier, 1980), pp. 91–92.

[32]R.D. Enright. "An Integration of Social Cognitive Development and Cognitive Processing: Educational Applications." *American Educational Research Journal*, 17, 1980, pp. 21–41.

moral development showed significant increases when compared with a control group.

Johnson, in a series of recent articles, has argued for additional attention to the positive potential of student-to-student interactions.[33] He summarizes many research studies which indicate enhanced performance in many types of school tasks by students involved in cooperative rather than interpersonal competitive structures. In addition to measures of learning, these students show increased cognitive and affective perspective-taking, enhanced desire to win each other's respect, and more frequent interactions across ethnic, social class, and other barriers. He also argues for the advantages of well-managed controversy in the classroom, compared to poorly managed controversy or avoidance of controversy. Among the characteristics of well-managed controversy are the open expression of ideas and the absence of an "I win—you lose" mentality. Through the creation of conceptual conflict, such controversy leads to enhanced learning outcomes.

Although little work has been done specifically on human rights education, in related areas it is clear that a teacher trained to facilitate cooperative learning, to value student opinion, to present a role model of one who respects the rights and opinions of others, to encourage students to reflect upon their experience and play with new ideas, and to give students some responsibility for control over the learning process can facilitate many of the learning outcomes which are important in human rights education. To include a global or international dimension in this approach may make it even more powerful. (For example, see description of twenty-seven activities suitable for international human rights instruction in classrooms with this kind of orientation in Torney-Purta, in press.)[34]

In fact, a British practitioner (rather than a researcher) has prescribed the establishment of a secure, supportive, open, and challenging climate in the classroom as the first step in an article entitled, "Life Cycle of a Course of Study on Human Rights." He suggests the following as first steps:

(1)   Establishing and valuing the knowledge and opinions which students already have—about fairness, laws, freedom, other countries, and authority.

(2)   Getting students to trust and respect others—to feel confidence that by expressing opinions they will not feel foolish.

(3)   Giving students a sense of initial self-confidence through the successful completion of simple tasks—listing questions about rights

---

[33]D.W. Johnson. "Group Processes: Influences on Student-Student Interaction and School Outcomes." In J. McMillan (Ed.), *Social Psychology of School Learning* (New York: Academic Press, 1980); D.W. Johnson; G. Maruyama; R. Johnson; D. Nelson; and L. Skon. "The Effects of Cooperative, Competitive and Individualistic Goal Structures on Achievement: A Meta-Analysis." *Psychological Bulletin,* 89, 1981, pp. 47–62.

[34]J. Torney-Purta. "Human Rights." In N. Graves; O.J. Dunlop; and J. Torney-Purta (Eds.). *Teaching For International Understanding, Peace and Human Rights* (Paris: UNESCO, in press).

which a series of photos raise, making a poster illustrating part of the Universal Declaration.

(4) Adopting a problem-centered and action-oriented approach to the subject by focusing on "problems to be solved" rather than "problems which overwhelm us."

(5) Giving students a measure of responsibility for designing and managing the rest of the course.[35]

The class then moves to a second phase in which many activities specific to international human rights are included.

Conclusions

Psychological and educational research has been cited in support of several propositions. First, a large majority of elementary, high school, and college students believe that certain basic rights are universally important and ought not to be abridged by governments. There appears to be a basis for human rights education in existing personal beliefs about human dignity. Second, American young people have a number of misconceptions about international human rights; many adults probably hold similar ideas. This is understandable since the topic receives little attention in most school curricula in the United States and infrequent coverage in the news media. Third, the timing of human rights education (in general) and the sequence of study of domestic, comparative, and international approaches to human rights (in particular) have received almost no research attention. An application of work in related areas leads to the statement of three principles, each of which has implications for timing and sequence, however. The primacy principle argues for the early presentation of international definitions of human rights (at the time of the first discussion of the United States Constitution, perhaps). The recency principle argues for the inclusion of analysis of current events in human rights education. The plasticity principle, supported by research on attitudes toward foreign people, role taking, conformity, and equality, argues that middle childhood is an especially appropriate time for effective instruction about international human rights to occur. Fourth, there is considerable research support (in other countries as well as the United States) for the value of an open classroom climate and student participation in the design of instruction, as well as cooperative endeavors in human rights education. These factors are even more important here than in social studies instruction in general, because of the danger of contradictory messages transmitted by proclaiming human rights in an authoritarian classroom or school setting.

---

[35]R. Richardson. "Learning in a World of Change: Methods and Approaches in the Classroom." *Prospects* (UNESCO), 9, 1979, adapted from pp. 187–89.

The research base for human rights education is not as strong as it should be. Nearly two decades ago, political scientists (including many graduate students) undertook research on domestic political socialization. International education in general and the socialization of attitudes and knowledge concerning human rights in particular have not received equal attention from political scientists (or those in other disciplines). In addition to further consideration of the questions addressed in this chapter, research is needed to evaluate the effectiveness of specific teaching materials and methods in human rights education and to investigate the relationship among concepts of rights at the domestic, comparative, and international levels. Groups of classroom teachers (as well as those who make research their business) could make important contributions to this effort to strengthen the research base for human rights education.

UNIVERSAL DECLARATION OF HUMAN RIGHTS

Education to strengthen respect for human rights

Article 26.   (1) Everyone has the right to education. Education shall be free, at least in the elementary and fundamental stages. Elementary education shall be compulsory. Technical and professional education shall be made generally available and higher education shall be equally accessible to all on the basis of merit.

(2) Education shall be directed to the full development of the human personality and to the strengthening of respect for human rights and fundamental freedoms. It shall promote understanding, tolerance and friendship among all nations, racial or religion groups, and shall further the activities of the United Nations for the maintenance of peace.

Chapter 4

HUMAN RIGHTS IN
ELEMENTARY AND MIDDLE SCHOOLS

Charlotte C. Anderson

Human rights is a terribly complex subject. That is why many people believe that only the more mature student will be able to grasp the intricacies of the institutional machinery and social processes which impede or promote those rights. Assuredly, these are complex, sophisticated understandings. But human rights education cannot stop—or, even, *start*—there. It must not simply impart knowledge. It must develop future citizens who have a deep-seated commitment to advancing those rights, as well as the capacity to act on human rights concerns.

In the early years of schooling, human rights cannot be treated simply as another ingredient in the curriculum to be taught, for example, between ten and ten-twenty on Tuesdays and Thursdays. Rather, the principles associated with human rights must permeate the total school environment. From the beginning of children's schooling, the climate of the school must reflect justice, security, equity, peaceful management of conflict, respect for group differences and individual integrity, as well as the other principles of human rights. Adults in schools must consciously strive to manifest the same behavior, knowledge, and commitments they are seeking to develop within children. Is this notion idealistic? Yes, definitely. Does it therefore have no real utility? Emphatically, no. Ideals are the best beacon lights humankind has yet devised.

Human rights education does not currently enjoy a very high status in the school curriculum in the United States. It is usually given even lower priority in elementary and middle schools than in secondary schools. Practically speaking, this means that one would not even be able to find the understanding of human rights and human rights issues identified as goals in most district curriculum guides. If this situation is to improve, some very practical steps must be taken. One practical step—and one which this chapter will attempt to take—is to embolden those educators who are already convinced that human rights education is a good thing. It is this group which needs persuasive arguments to convince a school board or curriculum committee. It is this group which will welcome suggested teaching approaches.

Human Rights and the Informal Curriculum in Elementary Schools

The informal curriculum of the elementary school offers a special opportunity to advance human rights education. What better lessons on distributive justice can children have, for example, than those that come from monitoring the water fountains to see that everyone gets his or her turn, or from watching larger children giving up the front seats in the auditorium so that the smaller children can sit there and thus be able to see the stage? Conflicts between rights also arise in the classroom—between the right of one child to speak and another to have his dignity respected. There must be an infinite number of such opportunities to promote human rights development in the typical school week. Such common, everyday experiences may seem far removed from the front-page headlines. But if children are not guided to develop certain basic perceptions and competencies through their everyday school experiences, they will not be equipped to deal effectively with the complexities of adult citizenship responsibilities in an increasingly interdependent and conflict-filled world.

An elementary and middle-school human rights program could have many goals and objectives. However, for purposes of demonstration, a select set of goals will be given here, together with suggestions for ways in which these goals can be effectively promoted through the informal curriculum and through various subject areas.

An international human rights education program in elementary and middle schools should develop a child's capacity to: (1) respect himself or herself, (2) respect others, and (3) promote justice.

Developing Self-Respect

If there is a keystone to a human rights program, that keystone must surely be the development of healthy self-respect and self-esteem in every child. Self-esteem should be sought for its own sake, but it also has payoffs for the child's understanding of the welfare of others, as well. Political socialization research has affirmed that a sense of self-worth and efficacy is fundamental to active participation in civic affairs. Further, socialization research indicates that without self-respect, there will be severe limits on an individual's ability to develop respect for others. If subsequent generations are to be able to take up the gauntlet and continue—even intensify—the human rights movement, both respect for others and a willingness on the part of individuals to involve themselves in the common good must guide them.

Self-respect cannot be taught in the same manner as biology or vocabulary skills. Rather, children seem to absorb it from school experience which reinforces positive feelings about themselves which are based in the family. School books which portray respectfully the other human beings with whom a child can identify can promote that child's feeling of self-worth. In the schools of pluralistic America, this means, for one thing, that school texts must convey the social, political, and economic contributions of all ethnic groups within the society. And it means that texts must portray the many historical "homelands" of the young Americans reading those books and the "homelands" of their ancestors in accurate, respectful, unbiased terms, thus conveying the message that "other people like me live around the world, and they—like me—are valued."

But, perhaps even more importantly, adults who show genuine respect for the child promote that child's sense of self-esteem. The child's sense of self-worth flourishes or withers depending on the patterns of adult-child interactions dominating his or her life in school and at home. Such patterns not only affect psychic growth, but shape the ways the child relates to others.

Introducing Children to the Declaration of the Rights of the Child

One strategy for simultaneously developing children's sense of self-worth and conveying information regarding international attention to children's rights is to introduce children to the Declaration of the Rights of the Child. Upper-level students will be able to read the original document with guidance, but younger children will need a simplified statement.

A third-grade social studies text treated the Declaration the way in which it is presented on pages 52 and 53.

(Although this lesson appeared in a social studies text, it is easy to see that it could be readily adapted to a language arts class. And in a creative arts class, children might write their own poems or songs of tribute to children or draw pictures depicting the various rights of the child.)

Children's Rights*

Another belief shared by many countries is the importance of children.

The United Nations drew up the Declaration of Children's Rights. These are the rights:

1. The child shall enjoy the rights stated in this Declaration.

2. The child shall enjoy special protection by law.

3. The child has a right to have a name and to be a member of a country.

4. The child has the right to grow and be healthy. The child has the right to good food, housing, and health services.

5. The child who is crippled shall be given special treatment and care.

6. The child needs love and understanding.

7. The child has the right to go to school. The child shall have exercise, fun, and play.

8. The child shall be among the first to receive protection and help.

9. The child shall not be hired for work until of proper age.

*Source: *Who Are We?* Third-grade text from the social studies series, *Windows On Our World,* Sara S. Beattie and Dolores Greco, authors; Lee F. Anderson, general editor (Boston: Houghton Mifflin, 1976 edition), pp. 203–204. Reproduced by permission of the publisher.

I am a child.
There are millions of children
    in the world.
The world belongs to children
    in a special way.
Because there are children,
    we know that the
    communities and countries
    of the world will
    continue in the future.

I am a child.
The world belongs to me in a
    special way.
Because of me,
    the world will go on.

Which of the children's rights
is most important to you?
What right of children would
you add to those of the United
Nations's Declaration?

Many worthwhile learning experiences focusing on the Declaration of the Rights of the Child can be devised for upper-elementary and middle-school students. For example, these students can be sensitized to their growing personal responsibility and efficacy in promoting children's rights for younger children by keeping a daily log of the actions they personally take to ensure the rights of younger children. These log entries will include such things as: "I took my little brother to the dentist" (Principle 4). "I did my morning patrol as school crossing guard" (Principle 2). "Helped my little sister with her homework" (Principle 7).

A broader international perspective can be promoted by viewing a film, "What Rights Has a Child?", which shows children around the world enjoying specific rights. After viewing the film, older students can monitor for a specified period of time newspapers and newscasts for examples of both promotion and violation of children's rights around the world. A New York State Education Department Project Guide suggests that students make a paper chain of thirty links, writing an Article of the Universal Declaration of Human Rights on each. Every day that a newspaper clipping is brought which illustrates a human rights violation relating to that Article, the article is hung with string or a clip from that link of the chain. The same procedure could, of course, be applied to the Declaration of the Rights of the Child.

Developing Respect for Others

Teachers can foster respect for others by designing learning experiences which: (1) increase children's ability to empathize, (2) decrease children's egocentric perceptions, (3) decrease children's ethnocentric perceptions, and (4) decrease children's stereotypic perceptions.

Dramatic first-person accounts of events and realistic portrayals of people living in other times and/or places foster children's *ability to empathize*. Having children role-play also helps them to internalize the meaning of human rights. Similarly, having children pretend that they are characters in differing social, historical, and geographical settings while writing letters, diaries, and newspaper accounts further develops their capacity to empathize.

The first steps toward *decreasing egocentric perceptions* are recognizing the existence of others' perspectives and projecting oneself into alternative perspectives. Perspective-taking is closely associated with the ability to empathize, and many of the same types of learning experiences designed to increase children's capacity to empathize will work toward decreasing egocentrism. The wider the spectrum of people a child has the opportunity to associate with, the wider the range of perspectives he or she will encounter and come to accept as legitimate.

The more limited children's personal experience is, the more vital it becomes that they experience such variety vicariously by reading stories and case studies of people from other cultural backgrounds. (See the annotated bibliography of children's literature in this Bulletin.)

Another and more personalized way of increasing children's sensitivities to others is by asking them to make a book which focuses on the ways human beings the world over fulfill similar basic needs. Here are directions for making such a book:

Have children make a double book using 8½ by 11 sheets to allow plenty of room for art work.

One-half of the book and one cover title read:

BECAUSE I AM A HUMAN BEING . . .

Page 1. "I need enough food to eat and a place to live. This is ME eating dinner at home."

Page 2. "I need to be loved. This is ME being loved."

Page 3. "I need to love. This is ME loving."

Page 4. "I need to do what I can do well. This is ME doing it!"

Page 5. "I need to know that I can look forward to a future—to being someone when I grow up. This is ME, grown up!"

Page 6. "I need to learn and understand. (I am curious!) This is ME learning."

Notation at the bottom of this page: "Now turn my book over and start again!"

One-half of the book and one cover title read:

BECAUSE MY FRIENDS ARE HUMAN BEINGS . . .

Page 1. "My friends need enough food to eat and a place to live. This is ME eating at A FRIEND'S home."

Page 2. "My friends need to be loved. This is ME helping A FRIEND to be loved."

Page 3. "My friends need to love. This is ME helping A FRIEND love."

Page 4. "My friends need to do what they do well. This is ME helping A FRIEND do this."

Page 5. "My friends need to know that they can look forward to a future—to being someone when they grow up. This is ME with A FRIEND, all grown up!"

Page 6. "My friends need to learn and understand. (They are curious!) This is ME helping A FRIEND learn."
Notation at the bottom of this page: "Now turn my book over and start again!"

Once the children have completed their books and explored all the various ways their own needs and their friends' needs are fulfilled, they are ready to explore why people in many countries believe that these are rights—things which everyone in the world should have. Younger students can find pictures of people in other societies whose needs (as identified in the children's own books) are being met. Such a search will soon reveal the wide variation in the ways these common needs are fulfilled.

The obverse of this, concerning the varying degrees to which needs are not met and human rights are denied, needs to be recognized also. Teachers will have to make decisions regarding children's abilities to handle examples of and issues relating to deprivation of needs. But, most assuredly, older children can and should be guided to see the relationships between human needs, denial of needs, and human rights. It is important, however, to give a balanced view of deprivation so that children will not get the idea that Third World countries have all the problems, while equity and justice reign over the rest of the globe.

Decreasing Ethnocentrism

Ethnocentrism has a decided tendency to rear its ugly head in human rights education. Even the best-intentioned teachers and curriculum developers tend to cultivate a certain ethnocentrism regarding human rights as they teach the principles upon which the United States is founded. We Americans are justifiably proud of our historical documents and institutions based on the principles of human rights. We rightly seek to engender this pride in our children. However, too often we also convey the sense that we—the people of the United States—have exclusive claim to these principles. President Jimmy Carter alluded to this national predeliction and simultaneously conveyed the more accurate perspective when he noted in his farewell address, "America did not invent human rights. In a very real sense it is the other way around. Human rights invented America."

Our children's pride in this country need not be diminished while their respect for others is enhanced. One way to decrease ethnocentrism while enhancing children's knowledge of key human rights documents is to have students study the Universal Declaration of Human Rights along with the basic documents of freedom in the United States. A simple study is suggested by a poster put out by UNESCO. On one side of the poster are listed thirteen selected articles of the Universal Declaration of Human Rights. Lined up next to this listing are corresponding excerpts from the Declaration of Independence and various amendments to the United States Constitution. Students can be asked to read the excerpts and search for similarities. The exercise also could be made into a game. Write excerpts on slips of paper and distribute them to the students. Ask one student to read aloud the statement taken from an American document. Then ask another student to read aloud a comparable statement taken from an international human rights document. The similarities which thus are revealed will demonstrate that many of the values which Americans cherish are values which are cherished by the international community as well.

Attacking the Tendency to Stereotype

Throughout history pejorative *stereotyping* has been used as an excuse for denying humane treatment to whole groups of people. Unfortunately, this tendency is still obstructing the universal recognition of human rights. Thus, any human rights education program must attack the tendency to stereotype. Unfortunately, schools may be inadvertently promoting the tendency to stereotype. Judith Torney-Purta has pointed out that stereotyping may be one effective way for children to manage the masses of data on foreign countries with which we bombard them in typical social studies classes. She suggests, "A teacher who stresses the relationship between peoples rather than exotic facts about them may make stereotyping unnecessary."

Stereotypes have two characteristics which children need to learn to recognize: (1) they are not true, and (2) they can get you (and/or others) into trouble. Children need to learn that if they search diligently, they will generally be able to find an exception to a universal and closed generalization about others. They also need to be aware that because stereotypes are beliefs, people who hold them behave accordingly—to their own and/or society's detriment.

The teacher who has laid a sound foundation in stereotype-testing, using rather benign stereotypes, can move to far more detrimental stereotypes—those that cut to the quick of the human psyche and support pathological social structures such as those existing today in South Africa. Stereotypes about ethnic and/or national groups can be brought out into the open in upper-level classrooms. By giving students access to a full range of data about each group, teachers will soon have students recognizing many stereotypes. However benign or malignant the stereotype, the basic strategies for correction remain the same. Pose the questions: (1) Is it true? and (2) What could happen if you (and others) believe it?

A Closing Note

The Declaration of the Rights of the Child declares: "Mankind owes the child the best it can give." What better way to honor that commitment and ensure that legacy for future generations than through a sound human rights program in the schools? Secondary schools can offer students opportunities to explore some of the complex issues of human rights manifest in our national history and current international events. But the elementary and middle school years are a time to begin nurturing the competencies and commitments essential to making the most of that later learning and to promoting human rights.

BIBLIOGRAPHY

Books

Abraham, H.J., *World Problems in the Classroom: A Teacher's Guide to Some United Nations' Tasks*. Paris: UNESCO, 1973.

Anderson, Lee F., ed., *Windows On Our World*. A K–6 social studies series. 2nd ed. Boston: Houghton Mifflin, 1980.

Buergenthal, Thomas and Torney, Judith V., *International Human Rights and International Education*. Washington, D.C.: U.S. National Commission for UNESCO, 1976.

Ferguson, H., ed., *Handbook on Human Rights and Citizenship*. Albany, N.Y.: Center for International Programs, State Department of Education, 1981.

Haviland, Virginia, *Children's Books of International Interest*. 2nd ed. Chicago: American Library Association, 1978.

Hutson, Harry, *Human Rights in a Global Age*. Bloomington, Indiana: Social Studies Development Center, Indiana University, Global Studies Project, 1977.

King, Edith W., *The World: Context for Teaching in the Elementary School*. Dubuque, Iowa: W.C. Brown, 1971.

Kohlberg, Lawrence, "Stage and Sequence: The Cognitive-Developmental Approach to Socialization." In *Handbook of Socialization Theory and Research*, edited by D.A. Goslin, pp. 347–480. Chicago: Rand McNally, 1969.

Morris, Donald N., *Teaching About Interdependence in a Peaceful World*. New York: School Services Department, U.S. Committee for UNICEF, 1975.

Piaget, Jean, *The Moral Judgment of the Child*. New York: The Free Press, 1965.

Rawls, John, *A Theory of Justice*. Cambridge, Mass.: Harvard University Press, 1971.

Remy, Richard; Nathan, James; Becker, James; and Torney, Judith V., *International Learning and International Education in a Global Age*. Bulletin No. 47, Washington, D.C.: National Council for the Social Studies, 1975.

Rokeach, Milton, *Beliefs, Attitudes, and Values*. San Francisco: Jossey-Bass, Inc., 1968.

Torney, Judith V., "The Elementary School Years as an Optimal Period of Learning about International Human Rights." In *Daring to Dream: Law and the Humanities for Elementary Schools*, edited by Lynda Carl Falkenstein and Charlotte C. Anderson, pp. 94–100. Chicago: Bar Association, 1980.

Periodicals

Branson, Margaret S., "Teaching Global Law: Law Around the World for Young Students." *Update on Law-Related Education* (Fall 1980): 24–26 and 47–49.

Lickona, Thomas, "Creating the Just Community with Children." *Theory Into Practice* 16 (April 1977), 97–104.

Merleman, Richard M., "A Critique of Moral Education in the Social Studies." *Journal of Moral Education* 8 (May 1979): 182–192.

Schwab, Lynn, and Falkenstein, Lynda. "Folklaw: The World's Peoples Have a Lot to Teach Us about Solving Disputes." *Update on Law-Related Education* (Fall 1980): 9–11 and 55–57.

Selman, Robert L., "A Structural-Developmental Analysis of Levels of Role-Taking in Middle Childhood." *Child Development* 45 (September 1974): 803–806.

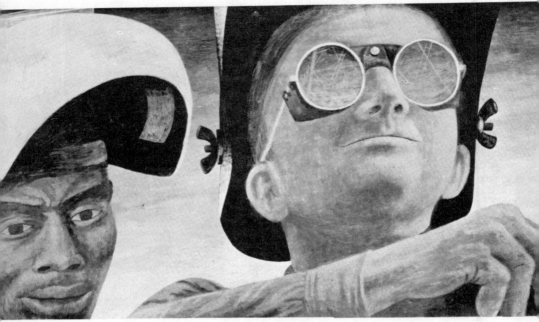

Welders. Ben Shahn. 1898–1969. USA. Tempera on cardboard mounted on composition board, 22 x 39¾, 1943. Collection, The Museum of Modern Art, New York.

UNIVERSAL DECLARATION OF HUMAN RIGHTS

The right to employment

Article 23.   (1) Everyone has the right to work, to free choice of employment, to just and favourable conditions of work and to protection against unemployment.

Article 25.   (1) Everyone has the right to a standard of living adequate for the health and well-being of himself and of his family, including food, clothing, housing and medical care and necessary social services, and the right to security in the event of unemployment, sickness, disability, widowhood, old age or other lack of livelihood in circumstances beyond his control.

Article 2.   Everyone is entitled to all the rights and freedoms set forth in this Declaration, without distinction of any kind, such as race, colour, sex, language, religion, political or other opinion, national or social origin, property, birth or other status.

Chapter 5

TEACHING HUMAN RIGHTS IN SECONDARY SCHOOLS

David C. King and Sharon Flitterman-King

In his farewell address of January 4, 1981, President Jimmy Carter aptly expressed the paradox of human rights concerns for Americans. On that occasion, Carter said:

I believe with all my heart America must always stand for . . . basic human rights—at home and abroad. That is both our history and our destiny . . . . America did not invent human rights. In a very real sense it is the other way round. Human rights invented America.

The fact is, however, that we Americans too often tend to see the question of human rights as an "international" matter only. We forget that a belief in basic human freedoms was the ideal upon which our country was founded, and that the authors of the Declaration of Independence saw those freedoms as extending to all humankind. "We hold these Truths to be self-evident, that all Men are created equal, that they are endowed by their Creator with certain unalienable Rights, that among these are Life, Liberty, and the Pursuit of Happiness."

The sentiments expressed in our Declaration of Independence are reiterated in the Universal Declaration of Human Rights, unanimously adopted by the United Nations some 172 years after Thomas Jefferson had penned the immortal words which set forth humanity's claim to inherent rights. The Universal Declaration opens with words that should have a familiar ring for all Americans.

Whereas recognition of the inherent dignity and of the equal and inalienable rights of all members of the human family is the foundation of freedom, justice, and peace in the world . . . .

Now, therefore, The General Assembly Proclaims . . . . All human beings are born free and equal in dignity and rights. They are endowed with reason and conscience and should act towards one another in a spirit of brotherhood.

Given the commitments to human rights which the United States has made, the need for citizens to understand and be concerned about human rights in both the national and international context places a heavy burden on our schools. We need teaching materials and teaching strategies which will help secondary students to see the relevance of the struggle for human rights to their own lives. Teaching about human rights, therefore, must become an essential part of citizenship training and that means taking its legitimate place in all areas of the social studies, not just in civics or government courses.

Considering Human Rights in United States History Classes

In our eagerness to get students into the vital subject of human rights, we often fall back on the few artifacts that seem to be readily available, primarily United Nations documents and the resolutions of international conferences. While acquainting students with these documents is important, we can inspire more enthusiasm and instill greater understanding if we make better use of the many opportunities we have in a number of "basic" or universally taught classes. Courses in United States history provide an obvious example. We can build a solid foundation for considering various human rights issues today by our treatment of key themes in United States history. One of the often-treated themes is that of our nation's historic sense of mission. A teacher might begin, therefore, by posing an initial question: Why did the American people develop a sense of mission or of a special destiny? Then, at every succeeding step in the unfolding of the nation's story, the teacher could use probing questions such as these:
(1)   At this point in our history, how did Americans interpret their sense of mission or special destiny?
(2)   What human rights were at issue in this particular instance?
(3)   At this juncture in our history, did all Americans share the same view of human rights? Who disagreed, and why?
(4)   Did Americans' sense of mission collide with harsh realities in this particular case? What was the result?
One understanding that will emerge from the consideration of the kinds of questions suggested here is that Americans—or a great many of them—did see their new world as the City Upon a Hill—a model that others could follow, a society based on ideals such as the dignity of the individual, and the rights to vote, to a fair trial, to be secure in one's own home, and to express unpopular views.

Of course, students will also notice that not infrequently Americans' actions seemed to contradict their lofty ideals and their sense of mission. There are many episodes in the history of the United States in which the interests of special groups have taken precedence over human rights. The destruction of Indian cultures, slavery, the obstacles in the way of women's rights, the problems of minority groups, Manifest Destiny, and imperialistic adventures—all are examples.

Rarely have we dealt effectively with these contradictions in the classroom. A decade ago, we tended to interpret those events in terms of guilt. That was not particularly helpful since many students did not know how to deal with feelings of guilt for wrongs committed in and by past generations. Today, we are more apt to go to the opposite extreme and gloss over those contradictions between ideals and actions.

A more reasoned and realistic approach is not only possible, but essential. Students need help in establishing some balance between condemnation and an acceptance or understanding of the forces that made such contradictions possible. We live with the same kind of contradictions today. Many of our students emerge from "global studies" courses with a sense that Americans are hypocrites, mouthing platitudes about human rights while supporting dictators or engaging in economic exploitation. Others come away from their study deeply disturbed by the revelation that the United States represents six percent of the world's population but consumes 35 to 40 percent of the planet's resources. How, they want to know, can we justify our standard of living, when millions live in property? And still other students may develop an unfortunate sense of superiority—we enjoy a high standard of living because we are somehow better than anyone else.

Until students learn to deal with such issues and problems, it will be hard for them to internalize any learning that we offer about international human rights. Developing an honest historical perspective will help, particularly when teachers are willing to deal openly with ethical questions and to encourage critical thinking.

Learning Activities for Social Science and Humanities Classes

In addition to the approaches just described which might be taken in United States history classes, many other opportunities for considering human rights exist in secondary schools. Ideally, human rights would permeate the entire curriculum. In reality, however, most direct instruction about human rights occurs in social science and humanities classes. The activities suggested in this section, therefore, are more suitable to those classes. The majority of the activities are based on the premise that social science and humanities teachers are accustomed to engaging in open discussion with their students. They are comfortable with the kinds of active, participatory learning experiences which the 1974 UNESCO Recommendation Concerning Education for International Understanding believes are most efficacious. For those reasons, each of the activities suggested here is introduced very briefly and then described in rather staccato fashion.

Activity 1

When students hear the term "human rights," what do they think it means? Prior to considering various definitions or consulting the Universal Declaration of Human Rights or other documents, ask the students for their understanding of the term. First, ask each student to make a list of the human rights that he or she feels are most important to him or her. Then, ask the students to rank them in descending order of importance, beginning with the number one and ending with the number seven or ten. Second, ask each student to list those things which he or she believes that no one should have the right to do. Finally, ask each student to write a definition of human rights in one or two sentences.

When the students have finished making their lists and writing their definitions, ask them to form small groups and compare their perceptions and definitions. Ask each group to identify common ground. Then, ask each group to establish a consensus definition of human rights. Repeat the procedure with the entire class.

When the class has arrived at a consensus definition of human rights, move to consideration of definitions offered by various scholars and in the International Bill of Human Rights. (See, Chapter 1, "International Human Rights: A Primer.")

Activity 2

Students need to become aware of the differences in the ways in which human rights sometimes are perceived in various parts of the world. Here is a very simple pre-test which could be given to generate discussion. This pre-test also could be used as a means of evaluating changes in awareness and attitudes, if used again at the end of a unit of study.

Pre-Test. Direction to students: This test will NOT be graded. It will be used only as a basis for discussion. Read each situation, then choose the answer that you consider to be the best. If none of the answers supplied seems correct to you, write your own answer in the space provided. Be prepared to tell why you answered as you did in the discussion which will follow this pre-test.

(1) The leader of the country was very proud of what he had done for his people over the last twenty years. The standard of living had been improved, children were being educated, and no one was hungry.
    "But," said the visitor, "there is no freedom of the press here. You only have one newspaper, and it only gives one view."
    The leader replied, "Some freedoms are more important than others."

Which freedom do you think he had in mind?
a. Freedom of speech
b. Freedom of worship
c. Freedom from want
d. Freedom of choice
e. Freedom from ignorance
f. _____

(2) Maria got along well with her Russian visitor, Alexei. But they did argue about differences between the Soviet Union and the United States.

"But you have no freedom in the Soviet Union," Maria said. "There is only one party in elections. Your newspapers are run by the government."

"We do have freedom," Alexei insisted. "No one goes hungry. Any person can find work. Medical care is free. Can there be greater freedom than that?"

What is the best conclusion to draw from that debate?
a. Alexei does not really understand the meaning of freedom.
b. The two countries differ in their ideas about freedom.
c. There is freedom in the United States but not in the Soviet Union.
d. People have greater freedom in the Soviet Union than in the United States.
e. _____

(3) A journalist from the Philippines who made a ten-day visit to the United States wrote: "The country is very rich, but the workers are badly exploited. It is clear that America could only have achieved such wealth and power by making certain sacrifices. The workers recognize that they must suffer so that industry can prosper."

What would be a good way for an American to respond?
a. It is always necessary for certain people to suffer in order for a country to advance economically.
b. The rich are generous in their support of charities, so their profits really help the poor.
c. The American political system gives workers important freedoms. They can elect representatives to protect their rights.
d. A visitor can only catch a glimpse of things, so he or she has no right to make a statement about how a country operates.
e. _____

(4) India's Prime Minister, Indira Gandhi, once said: "How can you expect people to care about the environment when their lives are polluted at the source?" In terms of human rights, what do you think her first priority would be?
a. Basic political freedoms, including the right to vote.
b. Environmental protection laws to stop pollution.
c. An end to environmental restriction in order to encourage economic growth.
d. Basic food and health care programs.
e. _____

(5) In 1958 the people of French Guinea declared their independence. General Charles de Gaulle, then head of the French government, warned them that they would suffer serious economic consequences. He urged them to remain a part of what he called "the community of France."

Sékou Touré, who later became President of the new African nation of Guinea, replied, "We have a great and pressing need. Our dignity! But there can be no dignity without freedom. When you are ruled by others, you are dishonored and turned into inferior human beings. We prefer poverty in freedom to riches in slavery." Which of the following human rights do you think Touré had in mind?

a. The right to own property.
b. The right to recognition as a person before the law.
c. The right of self-determination.
d. The right to a standard of living adequate for health and well-being.
e. _____

Activity 3

In this activity, students participate in a role-playing exercise dealing with the filing by individuals of complaints alleging human rights violations with international organizations (such as UNESCO). This activity has the important objective: to make students aware that UNESCO is one of the number of organizations which has instituted procedures by which individuals can file complaints dealing with what they believe to be violations of their right to an education, to share in scientific advancement, to participate freely in cultural life, and the right to information (including freedom of opinion and expression). Students are then given the UNESCO complaint procedures, material illustrating these rights, and a description of an alleged violation. They fill out the complaint form (Figure 1) with information such as: name; whether one is the victim or someone with knowledge of the situation; the human rights allegedly violated (referring to specific Articles of the Universal Declaration or the Covenants); connection between the alleged violation and education, science, culture or information; information about domestic courts consulted, and so on. Students are then assigned to play roles as a person or persons complaining of a violation, and as a member of the Committee (representing a number of UNESCO Member States) whose task is to examine the complaint, determine the issue and the facts, and decide what action should be taken.

After finishing the actual role-playing exercise, students are asked to consider questions such as the following:

• Why are rights such as these important?
• Why might some governments make laws which violated these rights for some or all of their citizens?
• In what ways can people complain concerning rights violations in their own countries?

This exercise can increase student empathy for those whose rights are violated, as well as teaching about international organizations which have procedures by which individuals can complain of violations.

Figure 1   **Form for Communications Concerning Human Rights To Be Submitted to UNESCO**

1. **Information concerning the author of the communication**
   Name _____ Nationality _____ Profession _____
   Date and place of birth _____
   Present address: _____
   Indicate in what capacity you are acting:
   ____victim of violation or violations described below
   ____representative of the victim or victims of the violation described
   below
   ____person, group of persons, or nongovernmental organization with
   reliable knowledge of the violation or violations described below
2. **Information concerning the victim or victims** (if author is the victim, go
   directly to part 3)
   Name of victim _____ Nationality _____
   Profession _____ Date and place of birth _____
   Present address or whereabouts _____
3. **Information concerning the alleged facts**
   Name of the country considered by the author to be responsible for
   alleged violation _____
   Human rights allegedly violated (refer, if possible, to the Universal
   Declaration of Human Rights, the International Covenant on Eco-
   nomic, Social and Cultural Rights, and the International Covenant on
   Civil and Political Rights)
   _____
   _____

   Connection between the alleged violation and education, science, culture, or information _____
   _____
   _____
   _____

   Facts of the claim _____
   _____
   _____
   _____

4. **Information concerning means of redress used**
   What steps have been taken to exhaust domestic remedies (recourse to
   the courts or other public authorities), by whom, and with what results?
   _____
   _____

   Has the same matter been submitted to another international authority
   concerned with protection of human rights? If so, when, and with what
   results?
   _____
   _____

Activity 4

This activity might be called an awareness-of-human-rights exercise. Its purpose is to make students more conversant with the basic documents of human rights at the same time that they become aware of the ubiquitousness of human rights issues in the world today. Students should work in pairs. Provide each pair with a complete edition of a newspaper. The teacher may ask the students to bring from home papers which are a day or two old. Alternatively, the teacher may ask a local newspaper to provide sufficient copies of day-old papers. Most newspapers are pleased to provide them. Then give each pair of students one important human rights document. Some students could use the Universal Declaration of Human Rights or the Declaration of the Rights of the Child. Other pairs of students could use the Covenant on Civil and Political Rights or the Covenant on Economic, Social, and Cultural Rights. Still other pairs could use the European Convention for the Protection of Human Rights and Fundamental Freedoms, or the American Declaration on the Rights and Duties of Man.

After each pair of students becomes familiar with the contents of the human rights document in its possession, the students should begin to examine the newspaper. They should circle the headline and the lead of each news story they find which speaks to a right mentioned in the document they have in their possession. If the article deals with the positive observance of that right, the students should put a large plus (+) sign by the headline. If it deals with a denial of that right, they should put a minus (−) sign by the headline.

When students have completed their tasks, let them compare their findings and discuss the issues respecting human rights which they have identified.

Activity 5

Positive as well as negative approaches to human rights are important. Awareness of violations needs to be balanced with some possible achievements, if students are to be motivated to work for human rights. In this activity, students are asked to project a future in which no more than twenty percent of the world's population would experience any deprivation of their needs or rights. In this future scenario, an institution with responsibility for human needs and rights would have been established and generously supported by the governments of the world. Students are asked to imagine that this Assembly of the Human Community would be operational about one hundred years from now. The students are then to look backwards from the year 2085 to consider how it would be possible to achieve this goal in each of the major areas of human rights. Suggest that the students consider such questions as these:

(1) Imagine that you are still alive in the year 2085. Look back over the

100 years from 1985–2085. Describe the kinds of changes which took place which have made the Assembly of the Human Community successful. Those changes may be political or technological in nature. Those changes may also be the result of certain important events which you saw happen in the preceding century.

(2) Describe the ways in which civil and political human rights are protected in the year 2085.

(3) Describe the ways in which social and economic and cultural human rights are being protected in the year 2085.

(4) Describe your part in shaping this future. What did YOU do to help make global respect for human rights a reality?

Conclusion

These teaching suggestions and activities underscore a major point about human rights education at the secondary level: human rights are not an isolated "extra," something to be stuffed into an already packed curriculum, but a concept that is integral to existing curriculum. Teaching about international human rights in our secondary schools is as necessary as teaching about who we are and the nature of the world we live in.

Much of this chapter has concerned itself with the "what" and "how" of teaching about international human rights. But there is another question—"why?" Why should we teach about this issue? The answer is as basic as our educational philosophy itself. One of the goals of a liberal education is to teach young people to think critically. By presenting students with an issue as multifaceted as international human rights and by encouraging them to analyze and evaluate its elements, we can develop this capacity in them. Not only is the subject matter inherently important, but its challenge to thinking critically about vital human concerns should make it an essential part of our curricular agenda. Only by developing such thinking skills can we effectively begin to prepare our students and ourselves for the world into which we are all growing.

Free to Travel. Rockwell Kent. 1882–1971. U
Pen and ink drawing, 1958. Collection of Ben Golds

UNIVERSAL DECLARATION OF HUMAN RIGHTS

The right to freedom of movement

Article 13. (1) Everyone has the right to freedom of movement and residence within the borders of each state.

(2) Everyone has the right to leave any country, including his own, and to return to his country.

Article 15. (1) Everyone has the right to a nationality.

(2) No one shall be arbitrarily deprived of his nationality nor denied the right to change his nationality.

Chapter 6

INTERNATIONAL
HUMAN RIGHTS EDUCATION:
THE CHALLENGE FOR
COLLEGES AND UNIVERSITIES

Jan L. Tucker

The Club of Rome uses the phrase "the world problematique" to describe the sudden realization of a world as a global system with complex problems and no apparent solutions.[1] Following a period of general optimism of the 1950s and 1960s, it appears not only that the world condition has substantially deteriorated but also that adverse trends are steadily strengthening. A major turning point in human history has been reached. Where does the United States stand at this juncture?

The Challenge for Colleges and Universities

With six percent of the world's population, the United States controls 30 percent of the world's energy resources. Within the United States, 20 percent of the people control 40 percent of the wealth.[2] Therefore, from one point of view, the national elite in the United States seems tantamount to a global elite. It is in the colleges and universities located in the United States where the great majority of global elite are being educated, including more than 300,000 foreign students. The policies and programs affecting the world's common global future are being influenced today by the education which these students receive in American colleges and universities. These institutions of higher education are appropriately conceived of as a global resource. This chapter will focus on the key contribution of universities

---

[1] James W. Botkin; Mahdi Elmadjra; and Mircea Malitza, *No Limits to Learning: Bridging the Human Gap* (Oxford: Pergamon Press, 1979), p. xiv.
[2] Jeremy Rifkin, *Entropy: A New World View* (New York: The Viking Press, 1980), p. 194.

and colleges to the achievement of a global perspective and describe the critical role of international human rights in building that perspective.

The record of colleges and universities in the United States in providing leadership in teaching, research, and scholarship to cope with "the world problematique" is discouraging. The curriculum of higher education is fragmented and only rarely includes interdisciplinary approaches to global issues. Most university leaders, from presidents to instructors, have had only very limited international experiences. Frequently, the competitive reward system of higher education causes faculty to disregard international interests because "there are more important things to study."[3]

The following facts underscore the problem in higher education:[4]

- Less than 1 percent of the college-aged group in the United States is enrolled in any courses which specifically feature international issues or areas.
- Only about 1 percent of college and university faculty members go abroad each year.
- Of the ten million students enrolled in higher education in the United States, only 1 or 2 percent participate in study programs abroad.
- Fewer than 5 percent of the teachers being trained today have any exposure whatsoever to international, comparative, area, and other intercultural courses in their work for certification.

Positive Efforts Are Underway

During the last half of the 1970s and early 1980s, education for a global perspective, including international human rights, was poised for a take-off. In 1979, the President's Commission on Foreign Language and International Studies issued its final report and called for increased federal funding for international education at all levels.[5] Several states, including Michigan, Illinois, New York, New Jersey, and Florida, issued guidelines encouraging global education program development and supported pilot demonstration projects.[6] In 1980–81, federal funding for international education increased by 50 percent, and the Secretary of the new Department of Education upgraded the status of international education within the Department.[7] In December

---

[3]Richard Butwell, "Why Don't Americans Study Anyone Else?" *The Christian Science Monitor,* May 28, 1980, p. 22.

[4]Rose Lee Hayden, "The World and You: Global Education Is the Answer," *International Brief Series* No. 6, 1979, Town Affiliation Association of the U. S., Inc., Suite 424–26, 1625 Eye Street, N.W., Washington, D.C. 20006.

[5]*Strength Through Wisdom: A Critique of U.S. Capability,* A Report to the President from the President's Commission on Foreign Languages and International Studies (Washington, D.C.: Superintendent of Documents, U.S. Government Printing Office Stock No. 017-080-02065-3, 1979).

[6]*U.S. Commissioner of Education Task Force on Global Education: Report with Recommendations* (Washington, D.C.: U.S. Department of Education, 1979).

[7]Shirley M. Hufstedler, "A World in Transition," in *Education and the World View* (New Rochelle, New York: Change Magazine Press, 1980), pp. 15–18.

1980, Congress passed a strong resolution favoring increased emphasis on foreign language and international studies.[8]

Although the effect of new federal budget austerity on international education cannot be predicted at this time, it seems certain that many of the seeds planted at the grass roots and in national professional organizations during the 1970s will grow and bear fruit during the 1980s.[9] The Education and World View Project sponsored by the Council on Learning is one of the major forces working to bring a global perspective to the curriculum of higher education in the United States. The World View Project bases its approach on the assumption that "academic institutions . . . must tilt towards the larger moments of human history."[10]

Education for a global perspective, which has achieved its greatest visibility at the pre-collegiate level, represents a significant force for change in higher education. Indeed, the effectiveness of higher education in the United States as a shaper of global futures may hinge on whether its curricula can be made to include a global orientation to serve both our own citizens and foreign students. Colleges and universities in the United States should be in the vanguard of the change process in global education. International human rights has an important contribution to make.

International Human Rights: A Necessary Content Strand

One criticism frequently heard in arguments against global education is that it lacks a content base. There are elements of truth here. International human rights, however, is one strand of content within global education that has developed a substantial mass of practice and scholarship within the past decade. Although other content areas such as food and population, environmental deterioration, and studies of war and peace have a significant research tradition, the body of information which exists in international human rights is only beginning to be recognized.

---

[8]H. Con. Res. 301 (96th Congress, 2nd Session, November 19, 1980).

[9]George W. Bonham, "Education and the World View," *Education and World View* (New Rochelle, New York: Change Magazine Press, 1980), pp. 6–14; Don Bonker, "Human Rights: Will Reagan Learn from Congress?" *The Christian Science Monitor*, February 25, 1981, p. 23; Barbara B. Burn, *Expanding the International Dimension of Higher Education* (San Francisco: Jossey-Bass Publishers, 1980); Richard D. Lambert, ed., *New Directions in International Education*, The Annals of the American Academy of Political and Social Science, 449 (Philadelphia: AAPSS, May 1980); National Assembly on Foreign Language and International Studies, *Toward Education with a Global Perspective* (Washington: Association of American Colleges, 1981); Paul Simon, *The Tongue-Tied American: Confronting the Foreign Language Crisis* (New York: Continuum, 1980); Marvin Williamson and Cynthia T. Morehouse, eds., *International/Intercultural Education in the Four-Year College: A Handbook on Strategies for Change*, Occasional Publication No. 22 (Albany, New York: The University of the State of New York, The State Education Department Foreign Area Materials Center and Council for Intercultural Studies and Programs, April 1977).

[10]Bonham, *op. cit.*, p. 10.

The important status attached to the International Bill of Rights by other nations has yet to enter the consciousness of many citizens of the United States, in part because international human rights matters are only rarely given much attention in the news media. Our interdependent world requires that we deal with other nations and people increasingly on a basis of equality, recognizing the global, political, economic, social, and cultural issues which are important to them. The standards governing these issues are embedded in the International Bill of Rights; and the decision-making mechanisms for protecting these rights are found in international and regional organizations, such as the United Nations, UNESCO, the Council of Europe, the Organization of American States, and, recently, in the United States Federal Judiciary System.

On January 2, 1981, as one example, the U.S. District Court in Topeka, Kansas, ruled that the federal government had exceeded its authority in holding a Cuban refugee in the federal penitentiary at Leavenworth, Kansas. The ruling was based on human rights that go beyond laws in the United States. The judge concluded that the Cuban refugee detainees have a "right under international law and the United Nations Charter—and a basic human right—to a rapid resolution of their status."[11] We can expect to find more and more cases based upon international law in our own domestic courts—confirmation of the increasing interdependence of the world and of the real-life significance of international human rights for our lives and for education in the 1980s.

International Human Rights Are in the National Interest

In an important speech delivered at Harvard University's 1980 commencement, Cyrus R. Vance, former United States Secretary of State, described the world of the 1980s as one of rapid change, growing expectations, better education, quickened communication, and diffused international power and intellect. Yesterday's answers will not provide tomorrow's solutions, and certain fallacies must be exploded. One of the myths that must be destroyed, according to Vance, ". . . is that there is an incompatibility between the pursuit of America's values in our foreign policy, such as human rights, and the pursuit of our interests."[12]

People all over the world want to have economic security, to live in dignity, and to be free from fear, from police arrest, and from torture. They want human rights. It is in our historic tradition and in our national interest for citizens of the United States to identify with these universal aspirations codified in the International Bill of Rights.

---

[11]"Judge Moves to Free Imprisoned Refugees," *Miami Herald,* January 2, 1981, pp. 1 and 17.
[12]Cyrus R. Vance, "U.S. Foreign Policy: Constructive Change," *Vital Speeches of the Day,* 1980, pp. 568–572.

International Human Rights as a Normative Framework for Global Education

The development of a global perspective will not *per se* bring with it a commitment to human dignity, social and economic justice, and cultural parity throughout the world. One possible result of global education in the United States, for example, might be support of a hard line toward poor nations and the poor within the industrialized nations. The pressure in this direction might become compelling if United States citizens, having newly learned about global realities, decided to maintain or even increase the current imbalance of resource production, distribution, and consumption—at any and all costs! Another scenario, one more consistent with the values expressed in the International Bill of Rights, would be growing sympathy with the global revolution of rising human expectations, in both its material and ethical realms, and support for the fundamental tenets of improved physical and psychological life for all peoples and nations. It is this latter path that former Secretary Vance recommended, and it is one which has widespread support among members of both political parties.

Global education, without the benefit of the content of international human rights, even within the social studies tradition of reflective inquiry, can avoid the tough questions that lie before us. Education about human rights explores these questions. In the face of global undernourishment and starvation, for example, shall food be considered a commodity to be bought, sold, or withheld for profit, or shall it be a basic human right? Shall individuals, as well as nations, have the right to register complaints concerning violations of human rights? Shall the population problem in the world be viewed as at least partially a problem of over-consumption of scarce resources? Shall human rights violations in one nation be criticized by another nation in the name of national rivalry or in the name of universal principles?

Global education with international human rights content does not ensure adequate solutions to these complex questions, but it does provide an opportunity for the questions to be given a fair hearing. The International Bill of Rights can provide a normative framework for dealing with the content of global education. The International Bill of Rights affirms the fact, not just the wish, that there is universal agreement about certain basic human attributes and rights.

The close relationship between global education and international human rights was recognized and confirmed in 1974 when UNESCO adopted the Recommendation Concerning Education for International Understanding, Cooperation and Peace, and Education Relating to Human Rights and Fundamental Freedoms. The 1974 UNESCO Recommendation defined human rights and fundamental freedoms as those found in the United Nations Charter and International Bill of Rights.

Reflecting the close relationship between human rights and education, its recommendations for the content of the new education called for the study of:

(a) the equality of rights of people, and the rights of people to self-determination;
(b) the maintenance of peace;
(c) action to ensure the exercise and observance of human rights;
(d) economic growth and social development and their relation to social justice;
(e) the use, management, and conservation of natural resources;
(f) the preservation of the cultural heritage of mankind; and
(g) the role and methods of action of the United Nations system in solving problems and possibilities of strengthening the UN.[13]

Clearly, so far as UNESCO is concerned, human rights is at the heart of education for a global perspective.

The Significance of the 1974 UNESCO Recommendation

The 1974 UNESCO Recommendation provides a set of guiding principles for the development of human rights education programs internationally, regionally, and nationally. In September 1978, UNESCO sponsored an International Congress on the Teaching of Human Rights in Vienna, Austria. The final document of the Vienna Congress urged that UNESCO create a six-year plan for the development of programs, research studies, materials, and implementation strategies. In June 1979, a group of experts under UNESCO's sponsorship drafted a long-range plan which was brought before the twenty-first UNESCO General Conference held in Belgrade, Yugoslavia, in November 1980.

Included in the six-year plan is the creation of an international clearinghouse for teaching human rights and for exchange of specialized research, as well as curricula and the existing courses in the field of human rights at all levels of education. Also on the agenda for the 1980s are working conferences, research, preparation of materials, and the study of new methods for teaching about human rights. A major UNESCO Conference is scheduled in 1982 for the purpose of reviewing accomplishments of the 155 member states with regard to the 1974 Recommendation.

The 1980s should be a fruitful period for international human rights education. Universities have an opportunity to be at its forefront.

---

[13]Thomas Buergenthal and Judith V. Torney, *International Human Rights and International Education* (Washington, D.C.: U.S. National Commission for UNESCO, Department of State, 1976). Available from Superintendent of Documents, U.S. Government Printing Office, Washington, D.C. 20402, Stock No. 44-000-01651-6.

Programs at the College and University Level

According to a 1979 survey of law and social science faculties of colleges and universities in the United States, there is considerable interest in higher education in the field of international human rights. However, in terms of actual courses being offered dealing primarily or secondarily with international human rights, the survey revealed "a somewhat disappointing situation."

Thirty-nine percent of the law schools responding offer courses primarily concerned with human rights, but only 4.5 percent of social science departments present such courses. The researchers concluded that international human rights education "enjoys a legitimacy at the college level, but that its realization is handicapped by competing commitments and scarce resources."[14]

For social studies teachers and educators with an interest in international human rights, these findings are discouraging. Most social studies teachers receive their content training in social science or history departments. The survey reveals that only one in twenty social science departments in higher education offers even one course in international human rights.

In order for international human rights in the context of education for a global perspective to become part of general education, global education itself must become institutionalized at the college and university level. Schools and Colleges of Education can and should exert leadership within higher education in order to advance the purposes of education for a global perspective, utilizing international human rights as a cornerstone. Colleges of Education are in the best position to perceive the need for change in both the schools and in the universities.

As one example, Florida International University, through grants from the U.S. Department of Education, has developed a comprehensive Global Awareness Program (GAP), which incorporates international human rights into the university's general and professional education programs, and, through staff development and inservice education, into the local school system. The GAP leadership comes from the School of Education, whose faculty works in close cooperation with faculty and administration in the College of Arts and Sciences, the University's International Affairs Center, and other professional programs in the University, such as those of the School of Technology and the School of Hospitality and Management. The program also has close ties with the University's student government association and local community groups, such as the United Nations' Association of Greater Miami and the Japan-America Society of South Florida. GAP is co-

---

[14]Richard P. Claude, Rick Krechewsky, and Jeffrey Love, "Teaching International Human Rights: The State of the Art," *News for Teachers of Political Science,* American Political Science Association, 27 (Fall 1980) pp. 1, 15–17.

sponsored by the Dade County Public Schools and the Florida Department of Education.

The program is designed to infuse international human rights issues into course content throughout the University and to stimulate awareness within the community. Course content has been revised to include international human rights, and new courses have been added in the School of Education and in the Political Science and International Relations Departments of the College of Arts and Sciences. Inventories of existing courses and resources are being taken in the School of Technology and the School of Hospitality Management in order to identify places in the curriculum where international human rights can be infused. The objective is to place content about international human rights into the training provided by the professional schools of the University, in order to develop an awareness of human rights in the policies and daily decision-making involved in professional and managerial roles, and to prepare social studies teachers to include international human rights issues in their classrooms.

In the Global Awareness Program at Florida International University, the content of international human rights is viewed as a bridge toward greater global understanding; it is viewed as a means, not as an end in itself. By the time external funding ends, international human rights will have become institutionalized in the University curriculum and learning programs on three levels: the university campus, the local schools, and the state of Florida.

The Catalytic Development Role of the University

Program development in global education, including international human rights, stands in sharp contrast to the packaged curriculum movement of the 1960s and 1970s. The new math, science, and social studies were generally developed apart from local school settings. Curriculum change at the local school level depended upon dissemination models that emphasized the importing of "expert" knowledge into settings where teachers, parents, and the community were largely "uninformed." Lacking any sustained and deep commitment at the local level, these curriculum projects eventually were shelved, and they failed to bring about any significant changes.

By contrast, global education appears to be most successful where educators, parents, and community leaders combine their human, material, and political resources at the local level. Global education is best conceived as a grass-roots activity. It has a potential for releasing human energies and resources to a degree unknown in the era of packaged curriculum, because people understand the need and become productively involved in their own settings. This local nature of global education requires, however, that university educators re-examine assumptions about program development and take a fresh approach to teacher training.

Staff development and teacher education in global education should be conceived as a broad change process. College professors need to see themselves as agents of change in the community—as developers of networks that require interpersonal and political skills, as well as content knowledge. Local networking is critical for the long-term success of global education. Federal and state grants in support of global education are extremely helpful, but they are most effective when used to support an existing network at the local level. Fortunately, these local networks and commitments appear to be increasing, thus promising that global education will make fundamental changes in education in the United States, rather than reflecting a passing fancy of a few hardy visionaries.

Conclusion

Global education, including education about international human rights, is here to stay; indeed, the universities and the schools may have to run to catch up. There is much to be done in higher education. Educators in higher education have an opportunity to marshal the energies of the grass-roots agencies and actors into productive and useful programs in education for a global perspective. The developmental task in education for a global perspective requires educators in higher education to be determined realists. That spirit is expressed well in a parable shared by a global educator from the Netherlands who has spent his university career in teaching a global perspective.

The Story of the Three Flies

"Three flies sit on the brink of a glass filled with milk. Fly number one falls into the milk and thinks: "I can't get out of here." The fly doesn't move and is drowned. It is the *pessimist*. The second fly is the *optimist*. It thinks: "What could happen to me?" It is all very easy. It begins to move wildly and gets its body covered with milk soon. This fly also disappears to the bottom of the glass. The third fly is aware of the seriousness of the situation, yet does not want to surrender without an effort to survive. It therefore thinks first of what to do. Subsequently, it begins to 'tread' milk. The result is that after some time it gets a solid ground under his feet. It has churned butter! The last fly is the *realist* who tries to view things in their real proportions and so has the best chance to survive."[15]

---

[15]Steven C. Derksen, Co-operator, UNESCO Center, Amsterdam, the Netherlands.

;9.º Necedad! dar les destino en la niñez

What a stupidity to assign them destinies in childhood.
Francisco Goya. 1746–1828. Spain. Sepia and india ink washes, 1818–24.

UNIVERSAL DECLARATION OF HUMAN RIGHTS

Motherhood and childhood are entitled to special care

Article 25. (2) Motherhood and childhood are entitled to special care and assistance. All children, whether born in or out of wedlock, shall enjoy the same social protection.

Chapter 7

READING AND "RIGHTING": BOOKS ABOUT HUMAN RIGHTS FOR CHILDREN AND YOUTH

Margaret Stimmann Branson

Do books make a difference? Indeed, they do! Human beings have known that for a long time—long before scholars began to do what now is called research and long before the Universal Declaration of Human Rights was written. For example, so great was the ancient Egyptians' faith in the power of the written word that they adorned the walls of the library they founded in Alexandria about 300 B.C. with an epigram proclaiming that its contents were "Medicine for the Mind." So sure were the citizens of ancient Thebes of the therapeutic qualities of reading that they dedicated their great library to the "Healing of the Soul."

Across the centuries, people the world over have continued to attest in various ways to their belief in the importance and power of books. Sometimes, they have exhibited fear of them. Time and again, self-appointed censors have tried to suppress those which they believe possess the power to "corrupt" readers. Time and again, tyrants have ordered books whose ideas they deemed "dangerous" consigned to bonfires. More often, human beings have given evidence of their veneration for books and the truths which they believe them to contain. Some individuals have dedicated their lives to the preservation or the teaching of books which they felt were of special worth. Other individuals have willingly put themselves in jeopardy while defending their own right and that of others to read particular works. A few individuals even have forfeited their lives, rather than retract or deny that which was written. To this day, people often make solemn vows and swear sacred oaths on books featured prominently in both secular and religious ceremonies.

The Importance of Books: Personal Testimony

Books have indeed been important to human beings ever since history began. Milton went so far as to claim that good ones were "the precious life blood of the master spirit." More recently, Paolo Freire, the great Brazilian champion of literacy, has insisted that even the "lowliest of peasants" has "the right to read" and thus to engage in "dialogue with the world and its events." Only through reading, Freire contends, is one able to "name the world" or to come to that kind of critical awareness which makes one truly alive, truly free. Like Milton and Freire, James Baldwin testifies to the importance of books in his own life:

You think your pain and your heartache are unprecedented in the history of the world, but then you read. It was books that taught me that the things that tormented me most were the very things that connected me with all the people who were alive or had ever been alive.

Any of us who ever has had even one "mountain top" reading experience knows how exhilarating it is to encounter a book which enables us to feel that we are engaged in a dialogue with the world, which connects us with all the people who now are or ever have been alive, or which moves us nearer to being a "master spirit." It is true that not all reading puts us on top of Annapurna, because not everything encased in covers is a book. As Charles Lamb lamented, some are merely "things in books' clothing." Fortunately, however, there are many "real" or good books. They are those which, once read, are never to be forgotten. They are those which touch us deeply. They linger in our memories. They disturb our conscience. They shape our dreams. They bind us to our fellow human beings.

The importance of "real" books and powerful reading experiences, particularly in the field of human rights, can scarcely be exaggerated. Reflecting on my own reading experiences, I have come to realize just how profoundly certain books have affected my thinking and my feeling about human rights. These titles come to mind immediately: *Cry the Beloved Country, Noli me Tangere, Andersonville, The Diary of Anne Frank, Child of the Dark, The Source, Pulga, To Kill a Mockingbird, Blossoms in the Dust, Beyond Dark Hills, The Gulag Archipelago,* and *Roll of Thunder, Hear My Cry.*

To read books such as these is to transcend the confines of time, geography, and culture. To read them is to be everywhere in the world, from South Africa to the Philippines and from the Soviet Union to the United States. To read them is to be at one with other human beings as they know despair, experience pain, harbor hope, struggle for justice, and, on occasion, triumph in spirit, if not in body. To read such books is to understand human rights in very personal ways, ways which no scholarly articles and no factual reports, however well-written or well-documented, can communicate.

Criteria for Selecting Books on Human Rights

Which books about human rights are likely to produce positive results? To compile the suggestions which follow, the criteria below were used, except in a few cases when choice was limited because little has been written about a particular subject area or for a particular age group.[1]

(1) *Technical:* The book as a whole should be pleasing in design. Wide margins and uncluttered pages are usually desirable. The type should be suitable in size and form for the audience for whom it is intended. The print should be sharp and clear. Illustrations should be meaningful, accurate, artistic, and in good taste.

(2) *Factual Accuracy:* The content should be accurate, unbiased, and impartial in its reporting of known facts.

(3) *Characterizations:* Where people are featured, they should be depicted in lifelike style to fit the era in which they are involved.

(4) *Correlation with Curriculum:* The content should support and enrich the curriculum.

(5) *Instructional Purpose Is Specific and Identifiable:* The purpose of nonfiction and "social message" fiction should be clearly recognizable to the reader and should contribute to an understanding of the surrounding world.

(6) *Plot:* Plots should have logical development and originality. They should deepen appreciation and enjoyment of literature, and stimulate perception.

(7) *Coverage of Material:* A book should not be so broad in its scope that it overwhelms the reader. Neither should it be so lengthy in its presentation that the size turns away the reader.

(8) *Coverage of Details:* The content should include the salient facts and should not digress too deeply into matters irrelevant to primary theme or plot.

(9) *Pace of Narrative:* Plot or ideas should evolve at a pace conducive to holding reader interest. Pace should be neither so fast as to reduce comprehension, nor so slow as to induce boredom.

(10) *Vocabulary:* The vocabulary should be appropriate to the student's reading level without compromising his or her maturity or interest levels by "writing down." The content also should include some words which will serve to enrich vocabulary.

---

[1] Adapted from criteria developed by Karl Hardin, Librarian, Professional and Schools Library Services, Kern County Superintendent of Schools Office, Bakersfield, California, Unpublished, 1981.

(11) *Presentation:* Information should be organized in a manner that builds on preceding information in a clear and straightforward way.

(12) *Style:* The style should be appropriate to the content, in acceptable grammatical form, clear, graphic, and sincere.

(13) *Adaptation:* Adaptation of books originally written for adults are acceptable, if they have a demonstrated appeal to children. Adaptations should not sacrifice the literary qualities which gave these books their original appeal. They should be well-written and in the same spirit as the original.

Apart from considerations prompted by the foregoing criteria, each of the books recommended here was chosen because it deals with one or more of the rights proclaimed in the Universal Declaration of Human Rights. It is impossible, however, to deal separately with each article, because of space limitations. The books recommended, therefore, have been grouped into three categories:

(1) *Books About Human Rights—Too Good To Miss.* These books speak to the larger spirit or the overall thrust of the Declaration and to Article I in particular.

(2) *Books About Human Rights for Younger Students.* While there are many fine books on human rights appropriate for mature readers, those which can be used with younger children are fewer in number and less well-known. Nonetheless, given what is known about the socializing process, few would dispute the need to introduce young children to the concept of human rights as early as possible in their development.

(3) *Biographies of Human Rights Advocates and Activists and Autobiographical Accounts of the Quest for Human Rights and Fundamental Freedoms.*

ANNOTATED BIBLIOGRAPHY

I. Books Too Good To Miss

Brecht, Bertolt. *The Life of Galileo.* Translated by Desmond I. Vesery.
    London: Methuen, 1965.
Dramatic treatment of one of history's most famous dissidents, Galileo. Brecht
asks the reader to see more than the historic incident. He draws parallels
between Galileo's time and our own. Knowing that he will be tortured if he
persists in inviting people to look through the telescope and transcend the
narrow orthodoxy of the time, Galileo pulls back. Galileo is depicted neither as
a hero nor as a persecuted innocent, but as a man of genius who is nonetheless
fearful. 14 and up.

Demetz, Hana. *The House on Prague Street.* New York: St. Martin's
    Press, 1980.
A *tour de force* that makes one recall *The Diary of Anne Frank*, yet has a
vibrancy and a poignancy uniquely its own. Helen, the protagonist, lived
through the Holocaust in Prague. She tells the story of her experiences as a
young girl, when she does not understand what is happening or why her once
happy, comfortable life and that of her friends and family are shattered so
irreparably. The language of an innocent person trying to comprehend barba-
rism makes this autobiographical novel a haunting one. 14 and up.

Fox, Paula. *The Slave Dancer: A Novel.* Scarsdale, New York: Brad-
    bury Press. 1973.
One of the ten books produced in the United States that was selected for
Honors by the International Board for Books for Young People (IBBY) in the
International Year of the Child, 1979. Effectively written, well-researched,
and sparkling with genuine characterizations, this book tells the story of 13-
year-old Jessie, a fife player on the New Orleans docks. Jessie is kidnapped and
made into a "slave dancer" musician on a ship involved in the nefarious slave-
trade between the United States and Africa. In the course of his impressed
service, Jessie witnesses and experiences gross violations of human rights.
When the slave ship is wrecked, Jessie and a black boy, Ras, are the lone
survivors. They meet an old man who treats them as sons, helping Ras to go
north to freedom and Jessie to return to New Orleans. Critics have called this
book "exquisite." 12 and up.

Frank, Anne. *Anne Frank: Diary of a Young Girl.* Revised edition.
    Translated by B. M. Mooyart, Introduction by Eleanor Roosevelt.
    New York: Doubleday, 1967. Other editions are available.
This powerful account of the two years that Anne Frank, her family, and other
Jews were hidden from the Gestapo during the German occupation of Holland
has become a classic. *The Diary of a Young Girl* is not a recent book, but it is a
well-known, widely read account of the Holocaust as witnessed by a teenage
girl. The book is the actual diary of this Dutch Jewish girl, and in it Anne Frank
records her feelings concerning maturation, love, and her perception of her
shattered world. Although the enormity of six million Jewish deaths is difficult
to comprehend, the agonizing existence of a single girl is an experience to
which many children can relate. Anne Frank went into hiding when she was

thirteen; her family was discovered and arrested eighteen months later. She died just before her sixteenth birthday. 12 and up.

Halie, Philip. *Lest Innocent Blood Be Shed.* New York: Harper & Row 1979.
The courage of farmers, peasants, and children during World War II transformed a small French village into a refuge for thousands of Jews. The villagers of Le Chambon rallied around principles of non-violence and brotherly love to harbor escaping Jews from the dangers of an intolerant Vichy government and a nearby Nazi SS division. 14 and up.

Hautzig, Esther. *The Endless Steppe.* New York: Crowell, 1968.
Winner of several awards, this book is a deeply moving, personal narrative of the period when the author was between the ages of 10 and 14. Taken prisoner by the Russians in 1941, Esther, her mother, and grandmother were shipped in a cattle car to a forced-labor camp. They managed to stay together and to keep each other alive in body and spirit through the severity of arctic winters and near-starvation. Told in eloquent language, the book is more than just the account of one family; it is a source of insight into the human condition and the meaning of human rights. 12 and up.

Kherdian, David. *The Road From Home: The Story of an Armenian Girl.* New York: Greenwillow, 1979.
A Newbery Honor Book and winner of the 1979 Boston Globe-Horn Book Award for non-fiction, this book is well on its way to becoming a classic. This is a first-person account, set in Turkey, and the story begins in 1907, when the narrator's mother was just eight years old. It tells the story of the mother and her people, the Armenians, who were threatened with genocide. More than a documentary, the account is filled with concern for humanity. It deserves to be read aloud as well as silently. 14 and up.

Lawrence, Jerome and Robert E. Lee. *Inherit the Wind.* New York: Bantam, 1969.
A powerful drama about a teacher brought to trial for daring to teach Charles Darwin's theory of evolution to high school students in a small Southern town in the United States. 14 and up.

Meltzer, Milton. *Never to Forget—The Jews of the Holocaust.* New York: Harper & Row, 1976.
First-person accounts of those who lived through the Nazi Holocaust. An eloquent, prize-winning portrait which examines human values. One of the ten American books selected for Honors by the International Board of Books for Young People (IBBY) for the International Year of the Child in 1979. Maps and a bibliography that lists 70 other titles increase the book's value. The author pursues questions which the Holocaust raised for people today and asks readers to join him in taking a stand for human rights. 14 and up.

The Middle Hour: Selected Poems of Kim Chi Ha. Translated and with an introduction by David R. McCann. Ithaca, New York: Cornell University Press, 1980.
The writings of Kim Chi Ha, a Korean poet sentenced to death, then life imprisonment, and held for years in a South Korean jail, at last have been

translated into English. His poems, written out of his anguish and suffering, manifest his belief in the ultimate dignity and worth of human life. The book closes with his powerful "Declaration of Conscience." 14 and up.

Orwell, George. *Animal Farm.* Harmondsworth, England: Penguin Books, 1977.
George Orwell ostensibly has written a fable about animals and the world in which they live. In reality, he has produced a searing indictment of totalitarianism and a sophisticated examination of the concept of power. Orwell once said that his central purpose in writing was to discover "how to prevent power from being abused." In *Animal Farm,* he sounds a warning for human beings in all countries to defend human rights whenever such rights come under attack. 14 and up.

Shaw, Bernard. *Saint Joan: A Chronicle Play in Six Acts and an Epilogue.* Harmondsworth, England: Penguin Books, 1968.
A dramatic account of one of the most famous political trials in history, and one that has special relevance for our own time. In addition to being charged with supernatural behavior, Joan is persecuted because she refused to conform to the traditional role ascribed to women of the time. With unusual effectiveness, the play explores the ideas and feelings of a number of key individuals involved in this event. 14 and up.

Solzhenitsyn, Alexander. *One Day in the Life of Ivan Denisovich.* Translated by Max Hayward and Ronald Hingley. New York: Bantam, 1963.
An important account of survival in a prison camp in the Soviet Union. Written from a prisoner's point of view. There is resignation, yes; but there also is an affirmation of the importance of human rights. Even in forced labor, Ivan learns that pride in the quality of his work gives meaning to his otherwise unbearable existence. The author warns those who are still free that they should be concerned for the defense of human rights wherever violated, because Ivan is—or could be—Everyman. 14 and up.

Spier, Peter. *People.* Written and illustrated by Peter Spier. New York: Doubleday, 1980.
Ostensibly, this book was written for young children. Or was it? It is a fascinating and whimsical celebration of the diversity of the human race and an unspoken plea for the observance of human rights. A book for all ages.

Testimony: The Memoirs of Dmitri Shostakovich as Related to and Edited by Simon Volkov. Translated by Antonia W. Bouis. New York: Harper & Row, 1980.
Denounced as a fraud by Shostakovich's widow and son, who still live in the Soviet Union, yet considered authentic by many readers, these lean, incisive memoirs present a scathing indictment of the conditions under which artists struggled in the Soviet Union yesterday and today. Selected as one of the Notable Books of 1981. 14 and up.

Ziemian, Joseph. *The Cigarette Sellers of Three Crosses Square.* Translated from Polish by Janina David. New York: Lerner, 1976.
This book, winner of many prizes abroad, has been translated into four

languages. A suspenseful, true story of a group of youngsters, some of whom were not yet in their teens, and how they managed to escape from the Warsaw Ghetto in 1942. They were able to stay alive by selling cigarettes, even though the Gestapo was nearby. The story, enhanced by photographs of the youngsters as children and as adults, is a testament to the human spirit and to the will to survive. The epilogue informs the reader of the survivors' lives up to the time of writing. 12 and up.

II. Books For Younger Children

Agostinelli, Maria. *On Wings of Love: The United Nations Declaration of the Rights of the Child.* New York: William Collins, 1979.
A beautiful picture book, filled with imaginative watercolor paintings done by a famous artist, Maria Agostinelli. The text in large print consists only of the ten principles enunciated in the Declaration of the Rights of the Child and expressed simply and directly. "Every child has the right to be protected from cruelty and unfair treatment" is one example of the manner in which rights are explained. 5 to 8.

Alki, Zei. *The Sound of the Dragon's Feet.* Translated from Greek by Edward Fenton. New York: E. P. Dutton, 1979.
Winner of the Mildred E. Batchelder Award for 1979 for the children's book considered the most outstanding of those originally published in a foreign language in a foreign country, this book was published first in Greece under the title *Konda stis Raghes.* It is set in pre-Revolutionary Russia, and the account is told with grace and humor by ten-year-old Sasha. Through her father and her tutor, Sasha sees how the human rights of other children less fortunate than she are denied. Although it deals with undesirable social conditions and the need for reform, the story does not get bogged down in its message, nor does it degenerate into a tract. 9 to 12.

Blaine, Marge. *Dvora's Journey.* Illustrated by Gabriel Losowski. New York: Holt, 1979.
The story of a Jewish family, harassed by the Cossacks, that decides to leave its native land and seek a better life elsewhere. The family's ensuing troubles and triumphs are seen through the eyes of a twelve-year-old. 8 to 10.

Bloch, Marie Halun. *Displaced Person.* New York: Lothrop, Lee & Shepard, 1980.
Stefan, a fourteen-year-old Ukranian boy, was ill-prepared for becoming a refugee. Nonetheless, he, like millions of other homeless non-combatants, had to struggle across Europe on his own in the final months of World War II. This book presents an honest picture of the cruelties of war, but it does more. It helps the reader to understand how a boy might feel caught up in the vast adult migrations of World War II. 10 to 14.

Chaffin, Lillie D. *We Be Warm Till Springtime Comes.* Illustrated by Lloyd Bloom. New York: Macmillan, 1980.
The story of a little boy's courage and his efforts to keep his mother and baby sister warm till springtime. It is told by Lillie Chaffin, an award-winning

author whose home and heart are in Appalachia, with love and respect for the peoples of the coal-mining regions of Appalachia. Poetic text. Beautiful oil paintings. 5 to 8.

Clark, Ann Nolan. *To Stand Against the Wind*. New York: Viking, 1980. A work of beauty and breadth which allows younger readers to empathize with a South Vietnamese family, consisting of three generations living together in mutual duty and affection, whose members' lives are disrupted by war. When those who survive are forced to flee, young Em must assume duties as head of the household and help others to learn how to cope as strangers in the United States. 10 to 14.

Coerr, Eleanor. *Sadako and the Thousand Paper Cranes*. Illustrated by Robert Himler. New York: Yearling Books/Dell, 1980. A moving and well-told story. Sadako was only two years old when an atomic bomb fell on her city, Hiroshima. Ten years later, she fell ill with leukemia. Sadako believed a legend that she would be well again if she could fold a thousand paper cranes. She had made 644 when she died at the age of 12. Her classmates folded the rest. 7 to 10.

Dear World: How I'd Put the World Right by the Children of Over 50 Nations. Edited by Richard and Helen Exley. New York: Methuen, Inc., 1979. Here are imaginative, sprightly, thought-provoking suggestions made by children around the world for "putting the world right." Every word in the book is written by children, and most of the drawings and paintings also are the works of children. This is a good springboard for discussion and an excellent basis for encouraging children to write and to solve problems. 9 and up.

DeRegniers, Beatrice Schenk. *Everyone Is Good for Something*. Illustrated by Margot Tomes, Boston: Houghton/Clarion, 1980. Based on a forgotten Russian folktale, this book makes a significant point about the importance of everyone. The narration is presented with understated humor and appealing illustrations which even pre-schoolers can enjoy and which will help them to think. 4 to 7.

Griffin, John Howard. *A Time To Be Human*. New York: Macmillan, 1977. The author of *Black Like Me* helps children to understand how and why prejudice dehumanizes those who are afflicted by it. This book is a powerful indictment of racism. Illustrated with photographs. 9 to 12.

Henderson, Nancy. *Walk Together: Five Plays on Human Rights*. Illustrated by Floyd Sowell. New York: Messner, 1974. Five plays concerned with freedom and equality for all. "The Pledge" tells of the Apaches and their right to live as they wish. "Harvest for Lola" deals with problems of migrants and their difficulties in education because they must move so often. "Get on Board, Little Children" is about the Underground Railroad and the right of everyone to be free. "Look Behind the Mask" concerns self-concept. "Automa" is a fantasy about children who lose the right to think and to make decisions. 9 to 12.

How UNESCO Sees a World for Everybody. Illustrated by Gian Calvi.
  Paris: UNESCO, 1979.
The publication of this large-format, brightly colored, and gently humorous
book was occasioned by the International Year of the Child. It explains in ways
understandable to children what UNESCO is, what it tries to do, and why its
work is important. 7 to 10.

Hunt, Linda, Marianne Frase, and Doris Liebert. *Loaves and Fishes, A
  "Love Your Neighbor" Cookbook.* Scottdale, Pa.: Herald Press, 1981.
This book sparkles with gentle humor while it guides young readers toward a
better understanding of their responsibility with food. It creates an awareness
that many of the world's children not only do not have birthday cakes and
holiday goodies, but that they do not even have milk, fruit, vegetables, or
sources of protein. It is an excellent vehicle for generating concern about
world hunger. Contains practical suggestions for helping others. 6 to 9.

I Never Saw Another Butterfly. Drawings and Poems from Theresien-
  staadt Concentration Camp, 1942–44. New York: McGraw-Hill,
  1964.
Young poets and artists who contributed to this anthology were some of the
15,000 children who passed through Trezia, Czechoslovakia, on their way to
concentration camps in the East. Only about 100 returned. The book is a paean
to peace. It does not moralize, because moralizing is unnecessary. The words
and drawings of the children who remember happier days constitute an
overpowering, poignant statement in and of themselves. 8 to 12.

Jones, Toeckey. *Go Well, Stay Well.* New York: Harper & Row, 1980.
The story of two 15-year-old girls who become friends in defiance of South
Africa's apartheid system, this book helps younger readers to understand the
human rights situation in that troubled land. Effective, realistic, and hopeful.
10 to 14.

*Kampuchean Chronicles: Narrated by Refugee Children in Words and
  Pictures.* Tokyo: National Federation of UNESCO Associations in
  Japan, 1980.
In April, 1980, the National Federation of UNESCO Associations in Japan, in
cooperation with the UN High Commissioner for Refugees and UNESCO, held a
drawing competition for children in two of the most crowded holding centers
for exiled Kampucheans. More than 500 children between the ages of 5 and 15
submitted drawings. The best of these drawings, along with excerpts from the
words of the children, are included in this slim, but powerful book. 9 to 12.

Kerr, Judith. *When Hitler Stole Pink Rabbit.* New York: Coward, 1971.
An autobiographical novel selected as one of the "Best of the Best" between
1968 and 1978. Its unusual title derives from the fact that Hitler's henchmen
confiscated all of this Jewish family's possessions, including nine-year-old
Anna's pink rabbit. The novel is a powerful statement about anti-Semitism and
the plight of refugees. 9 to 12.

Levitin, Sonia. *Journey to America*. Illustrated by Charles Lobinson.
  New York: Atheneum, 1970.
War and the ravages of Nazism take their toll on a family living in Germany in
the late 1930s. The father is the first to flee to America, establishing a home
where the family can be reunited; but before that eventually happens, the
three girls must survive a period in a displaced children's camp and learn to
cope with existence with different foster families. The themes in this book go
beyond wartime experiences to deal with issues of how human beings find
ways of coping with separation and loss. A moving account. 9 to 12.

Lobel, Anita. *Potatoes, Potatoes*. New York: Harper & Row, 1967.
Delightful and thought-provoking. The story opens with a mother and her two
sons who live in a valley between two countries. They "didn't want to bother
with the wars," so they build a big wall around everything they own and grow
potatoes on the rich soil. The mother thinks that she has safely excluded her
sons from the world, but in time soldiers come marching by. First one and then
the other son succumbs to the lure of gaudy uniforms and the "glories of the
military." One son becomes a leader in the Army of the East, the other a leader
in the Army of the West. Those armies, in time, become very hungry. They
return shouting, "Potatoes, potatoes, let's break the wall." Their mother
refuses them a single morsel until they lay down their arms. "Stop fighting and
clean up this mess," she orders. When they do, she lets them eat their fill,
whereupon the soldiers, now joined in friendship, shout, "hurrah for potatoes
and hurrah for mothers!" The soldiers return to their home to plant new fields,
but this time they do not rebuild the wall. The author/artist is a native of Poland
who now lives in the United States. 7 to 9.

Meltzer, Milton. *All Times, All Peoples: A World History of Slavery*.
  New York: Harper & Row, 1980.
A well-known historian provides young readers with an overview of slavery as
it has existed through time. He describes how slaves have lived in different
cultures and how they have fought—and sometimes died—to be free. Pictures
and powerful drawings add a valuable dimension to this account. 10 to 12.

*My Shalom, My Peace. Paintings and Poems by Jewish and Arab Chil-
  dren*. Edited and designed by Jacob Aim. Translated by Dov Vardi.
  First Published in Hebrew under title *Hashalov Sheli* c. 1974. English
  translation c. 1975. Sabra Books. Printed in Israel by Levanada
  Press.
Yearnings for peace and feelings on the experiences of war are expressed by
Arab/Jewish children. Children wrote and submitted the poems and paintings
in contests in Israel in 1974. The book is "dedicated in friendship to children of
the world." 6 and up.

Pelgrom, Els. *The Winter When Time Was Frozen*. Translated from the
  Dutch by Maryka and Rafael Rudnik. New York: Morrow, 1980.
Set in the Netherlands during World II, this story tells of a farmer and his wife
who take in any refugee who comes to their door during a cold, bitter winter.
At one time, they offer shelter to a Jewish family being pursued by the Nazis. At
another time, they help a young German deserter. At still another time, they
harbor a refugee suffering from tuberculosis. The story is packed with action
and drama, and the characters are well developed. 9 to 12.

Richman, Carol, author and illustrator. *The Lekachmacher Family.*
  Seattle: Madrona Pub. Inc., 1976.
The author/illustrator is a granddaughter of Krescha and Lois Lekachmacher.
Her book tells the true story of events resulting from their decision to leave
their native Russia in search of religious freedom and the right to live in
dignity. They and their nine children were Jews and oppressed in Russia,
particularly by the Cossacks. Not long after their arrival, the children were
orphaned in America; but the older children looked after the younger ones.
Charming illustrations with bright colors. Lively style. Suitable for reading
aloud. 5 to 7.

Seechrist, Elizabeth Hough and Janette Woolsey. *It's Time for Brotherhood.* Revised edition. Illustrated by John R. Gibson. New York:
  Macrae Smith Co., 1973. First published in 1962.
This book describes organizations and individuals that have worked to promote the concept of brotherhood and to further the observance of human
rights. Included is information about a variety of religious and charitable
organizations, civil rights movements, foundations, exchange programs, and
the United Nations. See the bibliography for additional reading suggestions. 10
to 12.

Simon, Norma. *All Kinds of Families.* Illustrated by Joe Lasker. New
  York: Whitman, 1976.
Though the emphasis in this picture book is on styles of family life in this
country, other peoples, including Eskimos, Africans, and East Indians, are
represented. 5 to 7.

Simon, Norma. *Why Am I Different?* Illustrated by Dora Leder. Chicago: Albert Whitman & Co, 1976.
This book is concerned with helping children to develop realistic self-images
and to accept themselves and others. It deals—often engagingly—with a wide
variety of differences in family lifestyles, languages, and hair colors; but,
unfortunately, it leaves out discussion of skin color, the most critical and
obvious difference. Despite shortcomings, this book is useful for launching
discussion and developing appreciation for diversity. 5 to 7.

Snyder, Gerald S. *Human Rights.* New York: Franklin Watts, 1980.
An easy-to-read and easy-to-understand introduction to human rights, written
especially for younger readers. 9 to 12.

Swados, Elizabeth. *Lullaby.* Illustrated by Faith Hubley. New York:
  Harper, 1980.
A delightful book to read aloud to preschoolers and kindergartners. Illustrations show mothers, fathers, and children from many lands and the ways in
which they express love for one another. The paintings vary in styles from that
of an Indian Buddhist to Chagall to African artists to early Picasso. 3 to 5.

Van Woerkom, Dorothy. *Pearl in the Egg: A Tale of the Thirteenth
  Century.* Illustrated by Joe Lasker. New York: Crowell Junior Books,
  1980.
Based on the life of Pearl, who became a minstrel in the court of Edward I of

England, the tale tells of the adventures of eleven-year-old Pearl and her brother. Together, they run away from serfdom to join a troop of traveling entertainers who teach Pearl to play the harp and to sing. 8 to 11.

Wartski, Maureen Crane. *A Boat to Nowhere*. Philadelphia: Westminster Press, 1980.
The story of a refugee family who leave their small village in Vietnam and become "boat people" adrift in the China Sea. Finally, they are given permission to land and begin a new life. The story is convincingly written and the characters are well developed. 9 to 11.

III. Biographies and Autobiographies

Archer, Jules. *You Can't Do That To Me! Famous Fights for Human Rights*. New York: Macmillan, 1980.
A survey of highlights in the struggle for human rights from ancient times to the present by a well-known writer of non-fiction. Bibliography. 14 and up.

Axelbank, Albert. *Soviet Dissent: Intellectuals, Jews and Detente*. New York: Franklin Watts, 1975.
A mature and objective assessment of growing dissidence in the USSR. Focuses on well-known individuals such as Solzhenitsyn and Nureyev, but also examines expressions of opinion about outside influence. Candid and provocative. Written by an eminent journalist. Extensive chapter notes. Bibliography. 14 and up.

Bernstein, Joanne E. *Dmitry: A Young Soviet Immigrant*. Illustrated with photographs by Michael J. Bernstein. Boston: Houghton Mifflin, 1981.
The story of Dmitry and his parents, recent immigrants to the United States from the USSR, who found their first year in America more difficult than they had dreamed possible. Dmitry's parents, a violist and an economist, were unable to find work. Dmitry himself was rebuffed by his classmates. A moving account of the problems commonly experienced by those who flee one country to come to another in search of freedom and opportunity. Suitable for younger children. 9 and up.

Bethell, Jean. *Three Cheers for Mother Jones*. New York: Holt, Rinehart & Winston, 1980.
An introductory portrait of Mother Jones and her struggle for the rights of those who labor. Suitable for younger children. 8 and up.

Cantarow, Ellen. *Moving the Mountain: Women Working for Social Change*. Old Westbury, New York: Feminist Press, 1980.
An oral history of three women activists: Florence Luscomb in the Peace Movement; Ella Baker, who helped to organize the NAACP, in labor and women's causes; and Jessie Lopez de la Cruz in the farm labor movement. Rich portraits of the women and of their times. 14 and up.

Douglass, Frederick. *The Mind and Heart of Frederick Douglass: Excerpts from Speeches of the Great Negro Orator.* New York: Thomas Y. Crowell, 1968. Adapted by Barbara Ritchie.
Douglass' speeches hitherto were available only in the four-volume work *Life and Writing of Frederick Douglass.* Now, the eloquence of this crusader for the rights of women, slaves, and American Indians is more readily available. The contemporary relevancy of what Douglass said about human rights is extraordinary. 14 and up.

Felton, Harold W. *Mumbet: The Story of Elizabeth Freeman.* New York: Dodd, Mead & Co., 1970.
Elizabeth Freeman, better known as Mumbet, was the first slave to take her case for freedom to the courts in Massachusetts in 1781. Unschooled but perceptive, she believed in human rights and fought for hers. Good for reading aloud and for sparking discussion. 10 and up.

Felton, Harold W. *Uriah Phillips Levy.* New York: Dodd: Mead & Co., 1978.
Uriah Phillips, who experienced prejudice because of his Jewish heritage, fought for the rights of sailors in the days of flogging, poor food, and tyrannical sea captains. 10 and up.

Hannam, Charles. *A Boy in That Situation: An Autobiography.* New York: Harper & Row, 1978.
A "Best of the Best" children's books selection, 1966–1978. It tells of Karl, who grew up in Germany in the 1930s and escaped to England during the Nazi regime. An honest, frank appraisal of human rights in a tragic era. 12 and up.

Hannam, Charles. *Almost an Englishman.* New York: Elsevier-Dutton, 1979.
A novel that continues the story begun in *A Boy in That Situation* (Harper & Row, 1978). Karl Hartland, a Jewish refugee from Germany, discovers that he cannot deal with his German past and decides to become as English as possible. He becomes estranged from his sister and other refugees who, in the past, have offered him financial and moral support. The book deals honestly with the problem of adolescence and estrangement from one's family and culture. 14 and up.

Haskins, James. *The Life and Death of Martin Luther King, Jr.* New York: Lathrop, 1977.
There are many biographies of Martin Luther King, Jr., but this is one of the more perceptive books; and it is suitable for younger students. The author not only recounts Dr. King's struggles for human rights, but probes his philosophy and his convictions about means and ends, as well. Selected bibliography. 12 and up.

Houston, Jeanne Wakatsuki and James D. Houston. *Farewell to Manzanar.* New York: Bantam, 1974.
A true and well-told story of one Japanese-American family's life in the Manzanar Internment Camp during World War II. 14 and up.

Koehn, Ilse. *Mischling: Second Degree: My Childhood in Nazi Germany.* New York: Greenwillow, 1977.
An autobiography of a young girl living in Nazi Germany whose part-Jewish heritage was hidden from her. Written with candor and integrity, the book's impact can be compared to that of *The Diary of Anne Frank.* 14 and up.

Laure, Jason and Ettagale Laure. *South Africa: Coming of Age Under Apartheid.* Illustrated with photographs by Jason Laure. New York: Farrar, 1980.
Another in the photojournalistic studies of young people in troubled, rapidly changing societies. Eight young South Africans from different ethnic, tribal, or social groups are interviewed to obtain their perspectives on the *apartheid* system. See, also, the Laures' earlier studies: *Joi Bangla: The Children of Bangladesh* and *Jovem Portuagal: After the Revolution.* 14 and up.

Niemark, Anne E. *Damien, the Leper Priest.* New York: Morrow, 1980.
A slightly fictionalized biography but based on primary sources and well told. Provides a portrait of Damien as a controversial activist, a hot-tempered man loved and admired by some and hated by others. 14 and up.

Reiss, Johanna. *The Upstairs Room.* New York: Thomas Y. Crowell, 1972.
Winner of national and international prizes, this fine autobiographical account tells of the trials of the author and her family in the Netherlands during the German occupation. For two years, the author and her sister hid in the upstairs room of the Oosterveld family, who themselves risked their own lives to protect the two Jewish girls. 14 and up.

Reiss, Johanna. *The Journey Back.* New York: Thomas Y. Crowell, 1976.
A notable book—sequel to *The Upstairs Room*—which describes the aftermath of World War II. 14 and up.

Sterling, Dorothy. *Black Foremothers: Three Lives.* New York: The Feminist Press/McGraw-Hill, 1979.
Portraits of three Afro-American women prominent in the struggle for human rights—Ellen Craft, Ida B. Wells, and Mary Church Terrill—drawn from new sources by an award-winning writer. Photographs and documents. 14 and up.

Von Staden, Wendelgard. *Darkness Over the Valley: Growing up in Nazi Germany.* Translated by Mollie Comerford Peters. New York: Ticknor & Fields, 1981.
This autobiographical account tells of a girl whose perspective on growing up in Nazi Germany is different from those whose human rights were being violated—at least at the outset of the book. The author, daughter of a prosperous and influential German farm family that is suspicious of Jews, gradually

comes to realize what is happening to her fatherland. A concentration camp is built near the family home. In time her parents are able to run the farm only with help from foreign slave laborers. Her mother, moved by their plight, tries to help them, only to be imprisoned herself by the Americans after the war. The story is candid and beautifully written, illustrating the havoc that violation of human rights creates in the lives of victims and perpetrators alike. 14 and up.

APPENDIX

UNIVERSAL DECLARATION OF HUMAN RIGHTS

Adopted and proclaimed by General Assembly
resolution 217 A (III) of 10 December 1948

Preamble

Whereas recognition of the inherent dignity and of the equal and inalienable rights of all members of the human family is the foundation of freedom, justice and peace in the world,

Whereas disregard and contempt for human rights have resulted in barbarous acts which have outraged the conscience of mankind, and the advent of a world in which human beings shall enjoy freedom of speech and belief and freedom from fear and want has been proclaimed as the highest aspiration of the common people,

Whereas it is essential, if man is not to be compelled to have recourse, as a last resort, to rebellion against tyranny and oppression, that human rights should be protected by the rule of law,

Whereas it is essential to promote the development of friendly relations between nations,

Whereas the peoples of the United Nations have in the Charter reaffirmed their faith in fundamental human rights, in the dignity and worth of the human person and in the equal rights of men and women and have determined to promote social progress and better standards of life in larger freedom,

Whereas Member States have pledged themselves to achieve, in cooperation with the United Nations, the promotion of universal respect for and observance of human rights and fundamental freedoms,

Whereas a common understanding of these rights and freedoms is of the greatest importance for the full realization of this pledge,

Now, therefore,

The General Assembly

Proclaims this Universal Declaration of Human Rights as a common standard of achievement for all peoples and all nations, to the end that every individual and every organ of society, keeping this Declaration constantly in mind, shall strive by teaching and education to promote respect for these rights and freedoms and by progressive measures, national and international, to secure their universal and effective recognition and observance, both among the peoples of Member States themselves and among the peoples of territories under their jurisdiction.

Article 1

All human beings are born free and equal in dignity and rights. They are endowed with reason and conscience and should act towards one another in a spirit of brotherhood.

Article 2

Everyone is entitled to all the rights and freedoms set forth in this Declaration, without distinction of any kind, such as race, colour, sex, language, religion, political or other opinion, national or social origin, property, birth or other status.

Furthermore, no distinction shall be made on the basis of the political, jurisdictional or international status of the country or territory to which a person belongs, whether it be independent, trust, non-self-governing or under any other limitation of sovereignty.

Article 3

Everyone has the right to life, liberty and the security of person.

Article 4

No one shall be held in slavery or servitude; slavery and the slave trade shall be prohibited in all their forms.

Article 5

No one shall be subjected to torture or to cruel, inhuman or degrading treatment or punishment.

Article 6

Everyone has the right to recognition everywhere as a person before the law.

Article 7

All are equal before the law and are entitled without any discrimination to equal protection of the law. All are entitled to equal protection against any discrimination in violation of this Declaration and against any incitement to such discrimination.

Article 8

Everyone has the right to an effective remedy by the competent national tribunals for acts violating the fundamental rights granted him by the constitution or by law.

Article 9

No one shall be subjected to arbitrary arrest, detention or exile.

Article 10

Everyone is entitled in full equality to a fair and public hearing by an independent and impartial tribunal, in the determination of his rights and obligations and of any criminal charge against him.

Article 11

1. Everyone charged with a penal offence has the right to be presumed innocent until proved guilty according to law in a public trial at which he has had all the guarantees necessary for his defence.

2. No one shall be held guilty of any penal offence on account of any act or omission which did not constitute a penal offence, under national or international law, at the time when it was committed. Nor shall a heavier penalty be imposed than the one that was applicable at the time the penal offence was committed.

Article 12

No one shall be subjected to arbitrary interference with his privacy, family, home or correspondence, nor to attacks upon his honour and reputation. Everyone has the right to the protection of the law against such interference or attacks.

Article 13

1. Everyone has the right to freedom of movement and residence within the borders of each State.

2. Everyone has the right to leave any country including his own, and to return to his country.

Article 14

1. Everyone has the right to seek and to enjoy in other countries asylum from persecution.

2. This right may not be invoked in the case of prosecutions genuinely arising from non-political crimes or from acts contrary to the purposes and principles of the United Nations.

Article 15

1. Everyone has the right to a nationality.

2. No one shall be arbitrarily deprived of his nationality nor denied the right to change his nationality.

Article 16

1. Men and women of full age, without any limitation due to race, nationality or religion, have the right to marry and to found a family. They are entitled to equal rights as to marriage, during marriage and at its dissolution.

2. Marriage shall be entered into only with the free and full consent of the intending spouses.

3. The family is the natural and fundamental group unit of society and is entitled to protection by society and the State.

Article 17

1. Everyone has the right to own property alone as well as in association with others.

2. No one shall be arbitrarily deprived of his property.

Article 18

Everyone has the right to freedom of thought, conscience and religion; this right includes freedom to change his religion or belief, and freedom, either alone or in community with others and in public or private, to manifest his religion or belief in teaching, practice, worship and observance.

Article 19

Everyone has the right to freedom of opinion and expression; this right includes freedom to hold opinions without interference and to seek, receive and impart information and ideas through any media and regardless of frontiers.

Article 20

1. Everyone has the right to freedom of peaceful assembly and association.

2. No one may be compelled to belong to an association.

Article 21

1. Everyone has the right to take part in the government of his country, directly or through freely chosen representatives.

2. Everyone has the right of equal access to public service in his country.

3. The will of the people shall be the basis of the authority of government; this will shall be expressed in periodic and genuine elections which shall be by universal and equal suffrage and shall be held by secret vote or by equivalent free voting procedures.

Article 22

Everyone, as a member of society, has the right to social security and is entitled to realization, through national effort and international co-operation and in accordance with the organization and resources of each State, of the economic, social and cultural rights indispensable for his dignity and the free development of his personality.

Article 23

1. Everyone has the right to work, to free choice of employment, to just and favourable conditions of work and to protection against unemployment.

2. Everyone, without any discrimination, has the right to equal pay for equal work.

3. Everyone who works has the right to just and favourable remuneration ensuring for himself and his family an existence worthy of human dignity, and supplemented, if necessary, by other means of social protection.

4. Everyone has the right to form and to join trade unions for the protection of his interests.

Article 24

Everyone has the right to rest and leisure, including reasonable limitations of working hours and periodic holidays with pay.

Article 25

1. Everyone has the right to a standard of living adequate for the health and well-being of himself and of his family, including food, clothing, housing and medical care and necessary social services, and the right to security in the event of unemployment, sickness, disability, widowhood, old age or other lack of livelihood in circumstances beyond his control.

2. Motherhood and childhood are entitled to special care and assistance. All children, whether born in or out of wedlock, shall enjoy the same social protection.

Article 26

1. Everyone has the right to education. Education shall be free, at least in the elementary and fundamental stages. Elementary education shall be compulsory. Technical and professional education shall be made generally available and higher education shall be equally accessible to all on the basis of merit.

2. Education shall be directed to the full development of the human personality and to the strengthening of respect for human rights and fundamental freedoms. It shall promote understanding, tolerance and friendship among all nations, racial or religious groups, and shall further the activities of the United Nations for the maintenance of peace.

3. Parents have a prior right to choose the kind of education that shall be given to their children.

Article 27

1. Everyone has the right freely to participate in the cultural life of the community, to enjoy the arts and to share in scientific advancement and its benefits.

2. Everyone has the right to the protection of the moral and material interests resulting from any scientific, literary or artistic production of which he is the author.

Article 28

Everyone is entitled to a social and international order in which the rights and freedoms set forth in this Declaration can be fully realized.

Article 29

1. Everyone has duties to the community in which alone the free and full development of his personality is possible.

2. In the exercise of his rights and freedoms, everyone shall be subject only to such limitations as are determined by law solely for the purpose of securing due recognition and respect for the rights and freedoms of others and of meeting the just requirements of morality, public order and the general welfare in a democratic society.

3. These rights and freedoms may in no case be exercised contrary to the purposes and principles of the United Nations.

Article 30

Nothing in this Declaration may be interpreted as implying for any State, group or person any right to engage in any activity or to perform any act aimed at the destruction of any of the rights and freedoms set forth herein.

DECLARATION OF THE RIGHTS OF THE CHILD

Preamble

Whereas the peoples of the United Nations have, in the Charter, reaffirmed their faith in fundamental human rights, and in the dignity and worth of the human person, and have determined to promote social progress and better standards of life in larger freedom,

Whereas the United Nations has, in the Universal Declaration of Human Rights, proclaimed that everyone is entitled to all the rights and freedoms set forth therein, without distinction of any kind, such as race, color, sex, language, religion, political or other opinion, national or social origin, property, birth or other status,

Whereas the child, by reason of his physical and mental immaturity, needs special safeguards and care, including appropriate legal protection, before as well as after birth,

Whereas the need for such special safeguards has been stated in the Geneva Declaration of the Rights of the Child of 1924, and recognized in the Universal Declaration of Human Rights and in the statutes of specialized agencies and international organizations concerned with the welfare of children.,

Whereas mankind owes to the child the best it has to give,

Now therefore,

The General Assembly

Proclaims this Declaration of the Rights of the Child to the end that he may have a happy childhood and enjoy for his own good and for the good of society the rights and freedoms herein set forth, and calls upon parents, upon men and women as individuals and upon voluntary organizations, local authorities and national governments to recognize these rights and strive for their observance by legislative and other measures progressively taken in accordance with the following principles:

Principle 1

The child shall enjoy all the rights set forth in this Declaration. All children, without any exception whatsoever, shall be entitled to these rights, without distinction or discrimination on account of race, color, sex, language, religion, political or other opinion, national or social origin, property, birth or other status, whether of himself or of his family.

Principle 2

The child shall enjoy special protection, and shall be given opportunities and facilities, by law and by other means, to enable him to develop physically, mentally, morally, spiritually and socially in a healthy and normal manner and in conditions of freedom and dignity. In the enactment of laws for this purpose the best interests of the child shall be the paramount consideration.

Principle 3

The child shall be entitled from his birth to a name and a nationality.

Principle 4

The child shall enjoy the benefits of social security. He shall be entitled to grow and develop in health; to this end special care and protection shall be provided both to him and to his mother, including adequate pre-natal and post-natal care. The child shall have the right to adequate nutrition, housing, recreation and medical services.

Principle 5

The child who is physically, mentally or socially handicapped shall be given the special treatment, education and care required by his particular condition.

Principle 6

The child, for the full and harmonious development of his personality, needs love and understanding. He shall, wherever possible, grow up in the care and under the responsibility of his parents, and in any case in an atmosphere of affection and of moral and material security; a child of tender years shall not, save in exceptional circumstances, be separated from his mother. Society and the public authorities shall have the duty to extend particular care to children without a family and to those without adequate means of support. Payment of state and other assistance toward the maintenance of children of large families is desirable.

Principle 7

The child is entitled to receive education, which shall be free and compulsory, at least in the elementary stages. He shall be given an education which will promote his general culture, and enable him on a basis of equal opportunity to develop his abilities, his individual judgment, and his sense of moral and social responsibility, and to become a useful member of society.

The best interests of the child shall be the guiding principle of those responsible for his education and guidance; that responsibility lies in the first place with his parents.

The child shall have full opportunity for play and recreation, which should be directed to the same purposes as education; society and the public authorities shall endeavor to promote the enjoyment of this right.

Principle 8

The child shall in all circumstances be among the first to receive protection and relief.

Principle 9

The child shall be protected against all forms of neglect, cruelty and exploitation. He shall not be the subject of traffic, in any form.

The child shall not be admitted to employment before an appropriate minimum age; he shall in no case be caused or permitted to engage in any occupation or employment which would prejudice his health or education, or interfere with his physical, mental or moral development.

Principle 10

The child shall be protected from practices which may foster racial, religious and any other form of discrimination. He shall be brought up in a spirit of understanding, tolerance, friendship among peoples, peace and universal brotherhood and in full consciousness that his energy and talents should be devoted to the services of his fellow men.

EXCERPTS FROM
RECOMMENDATION CONCERNING EDUCATION FOR INTERNATIONAL UNDERSTANDING, COOPERATION AND PEACE AND EDUCATION RELATING TO HUMAN RIGHTS AND FUNDAMENTAL FREEDOMS

The General Conference of the United Nations Educational, Scientific and Cultural Organization, meeting in Paris from 17 October to 23 November 1974, at its eighteenth session,

Mindful of the responsibility incumbent on States to achieve through education the aims set forth in the Charter of the United Nations, the Constitution of UNESCO, the Universal Declaration of Human Rights and the Geneva Conventions for the Protection of Victims of War of 12 August 1949, in order to promote international understanding, cooperation and peace and respect for human rights and fundamental freedoms,

Reaffirming the responsibility which is incumbent on UNESCO to encourage and support in Member States any activity designed to ensure the education of all for the advancement of justice, freedom, human rights and peace.

The General Conference recommends that Member States bring this recommendation to the attention of the authorities, departments or bodies responsible for school education, higher education and out-of-school education, of the various organizations carrying out educational work among young people and adults such as student and youth movements, associations of pupils' parents, teachers' unions and other interested parties.

I. Significance of Terms

1. For the purposes of this recommendation:

    (a) The word *education* implies the entire process of social life by means of which individuals and social groups learn to develop consciously within, and for the benefit of, the national and international communities, the whole of their personal capacities, attitudes, aptitudes and knowledge. This process is not limited to any specific activities.

    (b) The terms *international understanding, co-operation* and *peace* are to be considered as an indivisible whole based on the principle of friendly relations between peoples and States having different social and political systems and on the respect for human rights and fundamental freedoms. In the text of this recommendation, the different connotations of these terms are sometimes gath-

ered together in a concise expression, *"international education."*
(c) *Human rights* and *fundamental freedoms* are those defined in
the United Nations Charter, the Universal Declaration of Human
Rights and the International Covenants on Economic, Social and
Cultural Rights, and on Civil and Political Rights.

III. Guiding Principles

3. Education should be infused with the aims and purposes set forth in
the Charter of the United Nations, the Constitution of UNESCO and the
Universal Declaration of Human Rights, particularly Article 26, paragraph 2, of the last-named, which states: "Education shall be directed
to the full development of the human personality and to the strengthening of respect for human rights and fundamental freedoms. It shall
promote understanding, tolerance and friendship among all nations,
racial or religious groups, and shall further the activities of the United
Nations for the maintenance of peace."

4. In order to enable every person to contribute actively to the fulfil-
ment of the aims referred to in paragraph 3, and promote international
solidarity and co-operation, which are necessary in solving the world
problems affecting the individuals' and communities' life and exercise
of fundamental rights and freedoms, the following objectives should be
regarded as major guiding principles of educational policy:

(a) an international dimension and a global perspective in education at all levels and in all its forms;

(b) understanding and respect for all peoples, their cultures, civilizations, values and ways of life, including domestic ethnic cultures
and cultures of other nations;

(c) awareness of the increasing global interdependence between
peoples and nations;

(d) abilities to communicate with others;

(e) awareness not only of the rights but also of the duties incumbent
upon individuals, social groups and nations towards each other;

(f) understanding of the necessity for international solidarity and
co-operation;

(g) readiness on the part of the individual to participate in solving
the problems of his community, his country and the world at large.

5. Combining learning, training, information and action, international
education should further the appropriate intellectual and emotional
development of the individual. It should develop a sense of social
responsibility and of solidarity with less privileged groups and should
lead to observance of the principles of equality in everyday conduct. It
should also help to develop qualities, aptitudes and abilities which
enable the individual to acquire a critical understanding of problems
at the national and the international level; to understand and explain

facts, opinions and ideas; to work in a group; to accept and participate in free discussions; to observe the elementary rules of procedure applicable to any discussion; and to base value-judgements and decisions on a rational analysis of relevant facts and factors.

6. Education should stress the inadmissibility of recourse to war for purposes of expansion, aggression and domination, or to the use of force and violence for purposes of repression, and should bring every person to understand and assume his or her responsibilities for the maintenance of peace. It should contribute to international understanding and strengthening of world peace and to the activities in the struggle against colonialism and neo-colonialism in all their forms and manifestations, and against all forms and varieties of racialism, fascism, and apartheid as well as other ideologies which breed national and racial hatred and which are contrary to the purposes of this recommendation.

V. Particular Aspects of Learning, Training and Action

Ethical and civic aspects

10. Member States should take appropriate steps to strengthen and develop in the processes of learning and training, attitudes and behaviour based on recognition of the equality and necessary interdependence of nations and peoples.

11. Member States should take steps to ensure that the principles of the Universal Declaration of Human Rights and of the International Convention on the Elimination of All Forms of Racial Discrimination become an integral part of the developing personality of each child, adolescent, young person or adult by applying these principles in the daily conduct of education at each level and in all its forms, thus enabling each individual to contribute personally to the regeneration and extension of education in the direction indicated.

VII. Teacher Preparation

33. Member States should constantly improve the ways and means of preparing and certifying teachers and other educational personnel for their role in pursuing the objectives of this recommendation and should, to this end:

(a) provide teachers with motivations for their subsequent work: commitment to the ethics of human rights and to the aim of changing society, so that human rights are applied in practice; a grasp of the fundamental unity of mankind; ability to instill appreciation of the riches which the diversity of cultures can bestow on every individual, group or nation;

(b) provide basic interdisciplinary knowledge of world problems and the problems of international co-operation, through, among other means, work to solve these problems.

INDEX

A

American Convention on Human Rights (the "Pact of San José"), 11, 17.
American Declaration on the Rights and Duties of Man, 17, 68.
American Revolution, 8.
Amnesty International, 18, 38.
Apartheid, 9, 38.
Armaments, 38.

B

Bilingual Education Act, 23.
Bilingual studies, 23, 24.
Bill of Rights, 1, 26, 31, 33.

C

Carter, Jimmy, 56, 61.
Center for Global Perspectives, 29.
Children, rights of, 19. See also Declaration of the Rights of the Child.
Citizenship education, 1, 4, 23–33, 35, 50, 62.
Civic education, 23–33, 36.
Cognitive distortion, 42.
Commission on Foreign Language and International Studies, 31, 72.
Commission on Human Rights, 10, 12, 15, 16.
Committee of Foreign Ministers, 17.
Committee on the Elimination of Racial Discrimination, 19.
Conflict management, 49.
Conformity, 41.
Council of Europe, 16, 74.
Council on Learning, 37, 73.
Cultural pluralism. See Pluralism.

D

De Gaulle, Charles, 65.
Declaration of Independence, 10, 57, 61.
Declaration of the Rights of a Child, 5, 19, 51, 52, 54, 58, 68.
Due Process, 2.

E

Education, right to, 3, 14, 38, 64.
Education and World View Project, 73.
Educational Testing Service, 37, 38.
Egocentrism, 54.
Elementary and Secondary Education Act, 24.
Empathy, 54, 66.
Environmental pollution, 38, 65.
Equity, 41, 42, 49, 56.
Ethnic Heritage Studies Act, 23.
Ethnic minorities, rights of, 19. See also Racial discrimination.
Ethnic studies, 24.
Ethnocentrism, 54, 56.
European Convention for the Protection of Human Rights and Fundamental Freedoms, 16, 17, 68.
European Court of Human Rights, 17.
European Human Rights Commission, 16, 17.

F

French Revolution, 8.

G

Gandhi, Indira, 65.
Global Awareness Program (GAP), 77–78.
Global education, 1, 4, 5, 23–33, 35, 71–79. See also International education.
Global system, 71.

H

Helsinki Agreement, 11.
"Higher law," 8.
Holocaust, 3, 30.
Human Rights Committee, 16.
Hunger, 3, 5, 9, 38, 64, 65.

I

Illiteracy, 10.
Inflation, 38.
Inter-American Commission on Human Rights, 17.
Inter-American Court of Human Rights, 17.
International Bill of Rights, 14, 15, 64, 74, 75.
International Commission of Jurists, 18.
International Committee of the Red Cross, 17, 18.
International Congress on the Teaching of Human Rights, 76.
International Convention on the Elimination of All Forms of Racial Discrimination, 19.
International Covenant on Civil and Political Rights, 5, 7, 11, 14, 15, 16, 31, 67, 68.
International Covenant on Economic, Social, and Cultural Rights, 5, 7, 11, 14, 15, 16, 31, 67, 68.
International education, 23–33, 73. *See also* Global education.
International Education Act of 1966, 29.
International law, 3.
International League for Human Rights, 18.
International Year of the Child, 19.

J

Jefferson, Thomas, 61.
Johnson, Lyndon, 30.
"Just civic community," 26.
Justice, 42, 49, 50, 56, 61.

L

Law-related education, 1.
Law-Related Education Act, 24.
League of Nations, 38.

M

Manifest Destiny, 63.
Mershon Center at the Ohio State University, 29.

Mid-America Program in Bloomington, Indiana, 29.
Minority problems, 63. *See also* Ethnic minorities, rights of.
Multicultural education, 23, 24, 26, 31, 32.

N

National Assessment of Educational Progress, 38, 40.
National Defense Education Act of 1958, 29.
Natural law, 8.
New York State Education Department Project Guide, 54.
Nongovernmental organizations (NGOs), 17, 18.

O

Optional Protocol to the Covenant on Civil and Political Rights, 15, 16.
Organization of American States (OAS), 11, 17, 74.
Overpopulation, 38.

P

Perspective-taking, 54.
Plasticity principle, 39, 40, 41, 43, 46.
Pluralism, 23, 25, 26, 27, 31, 32, 51.
Political freedom, 37, 65, 69.
Press, freedom of the, 64.
Primacy principle, 39, 46.

R

Racial discrimination, 19, 36. *See also* Minority problems.
Recency principle, 39, 40, 46.
Recommendation Concerning Education for International Understanding, Co-operation and Peace and Education Relating to Human Rights and Fundamental Freedoms, 4, 23, 31, 63–64, 75, 76.
Red Cross, *See* International Committee of the Red Cross.

Religious discrimination, 36.
Role-playing, 54, 66.

S

Self-esteem, 50, 51.
Self-respect, 50, 51.
Self-worth, 51.
Speech, freedom of, 2.
Stereotyping, 41, 43, 54, 57.
Strike, right to, 3.

T

Teacher Corps Act, 23.
Third World, 56.

U

Unions, trade, 3, 30.
United Nations, 3, 11, 12, 14, 15, 16, 18, 19, 38, 61, 62, 74, 76.
United Nations Charter, 3, 7, 11, 12, 13, 14, 15, 74, 75.
United Nations Children's Fund (UNICEF), 19.
United Nations Commission on the Status of Women, 15, 19.

United Nations Educational, Scientific, and Cultural Organization (UNESCO), 1, 4, 15, 23, 31, 56, 63, 66, 67, 74, 75, 76.
United States Constitution, 1, 2, 3, 11, 26, 31, 32, 40, 57.
United States Federal Judiciary System, 74.
United States history courses, 62, 63.
Universal Declaration of Human Rights, 3, 5, 7, 11, 12, 13, 14, 15, 16, 20, 21, 31, 36, 38, 40, 43, 44, 56, 57, 61, 64, 66, 67, 68.

V

Vance, Cyrus R., 74, 75.
Vietnam War, 25.
Voting, freedom of, 2.

W

War, 38.
Watergate affair, 25.
Women, rights of, 19, 36, 63.
Work, right to, 3, 65.

OTHER NCSS PUBLICATIONS
OF SPECIAL INTEREST

498-15278 FUTURES UNLIMITED:
TEACHING ABOUT WORLDS TO COME

Robert M. Fitch and Cordell M. Svengalis
Bulletin 59. Provides a theoretical framework and practical suggestions for teachers planning to teach about the future. 1979. 88 pp. $7.25.

498-15280 TEACHING SOCIAL STUDIES
IN OTHER NATIONS

Howard D. Mehlinger and Jan L. Tucker, Editors
Bulletin 60. Up-to-date analysis of social studies education in England, the Federal Republic of Germany, Japan, Nigeria, and Thailand. 1979. 104 pp. $7.25.

498-15252 INTERNATIONAL LEARNING
AND INTERNATIONAL EDUCATION
IN A GLOBAL AGE

Richard C. Remy, James A. Nathan, James M. Becker, and Judith V. Torney
Bulletin 47. Examines ways to learn about the world, alternative views of the world, and designs for world studies programs. Bibliography and Guidelines, 1975. 104 pp. $6.95.

SOCIAL EDUCATION, journal of the
National Council for the Social Studies

Back issues are available from October 1977, $1.50 each. Material on Global Education appears in the issues for January 1977, October 1978, October 1979, and March 1980.

DATE DUE

DATE DUE			
FEB 10 '87			
APR 21 '87			
			PRINTED IN U.S.A.